LOST SKI AREAS
of
Southern California

I0809479

INGRID P. WICKEN

Foreword by Doug Pfeiffer

The History PRESS

Published by The History Press
Charleston, SC 29403
www.historypress.net

First published 2012

Manufactured in the United States

ISBN 978.1.60949.387.5

Library of Congress CIP data applied for.

Notice: The information in this book is true and complete to the best of our knowledge. It is offered without guarantee on the part of the author or The History Press. The author and The History Press disclaim all liability in connection with the use of this book.

For Kathy

CONTENTS

FOREWORD

This book is fascinating. It reveals that we skiers have ghosts in our midst. Not people ghosts, not ghost towns, but place ghosts—ski-area ghosts, places where, in the 1930s, '40s, '50s and even '60s at least a short rope tow provided an up-ski for more down-ski thrills and delights. These spots have now mostly slipped out of memory and perhaps left no vestiges of their once fun-filled snow-bound existence.

In a few places described in the pages of this enchanting recapitulation of ski days gone by, there, high up on the trunk of a thick-barked Jefferson pine or white fir, hangs a metal wheel, the tire rim off some old vehicle. Once upon a time, such skeletal remnants provided a means for the return portion for the tow rope. They are there for all ghost busters to see, to reminisce, to savor old pleasures. Now, obscured by branches and often many feet higher up on the tree trunks than originally, they may be hard to spot. I know of at least one not far from my home in Big Bear Lake, at a ski site once known as the Upper Mill Creek Ski Area.

The author of this important book, Ingrid Wicken, brings such ghost areas back to life, especially for those of us who snowplowed, stemmed, christied and tumbled on their often short and gentle hills—and, it seemed, had our arms pulled from our shoulder sockets by those all-too-often soggy, writhing rope tows. But wasn't it fun, especially as we tell tales to young listeners!

In an important way, this book is a sequel to Wicken's first book, *Pray for Snow: The History of Skiing in Southern California* (Vasa Press, 2002). That is a book about the people and skiing sites of these times. It is fascinating to reread it and compare today with the ghosts of the past: names of pioneers like Walter Mosauer, Wolfgang Lert, Sverre Engen, Johnny Elvrum, Tommi Tyndall, Herb Leffler, Lynn Newcomb, Sepp Benedikter and Howard More, to name but a few of skiing's foresighted pioneers who pop up in the pages of both books.

A few ghost ski areas grew into good-sized modern ski resorts. Witness, for example, Big Bear's Snow Summit and Bear Mountain. The latter was originally a small "one-rope hill" called Moonridge Ski Area. Snow Summit once operated with rope tows only, not the twelve or so chairlifts of today. Wrightwood's Mountain High complex was once several ski areas—Table Mountain, Blue Ridge and Holiday Hill—all in the region known as Big Pines, where, especially in the '30s, world record ski jumps were established. Even Snow Valley west of Big Bear was originally a small center known as Fish Camp and pioneered by Norwegian ski jumping stalwart Sverre Engen.

Skier, professor of kinesiology at Moreno Valley College, historian and author Ingrid Wicken has done it again, this time creating another great book capturing the amazing saga of skiing in this improbable ski country of Southern California—improbable because this region is most often thought of as being the home of sunshine, orange groves, beaches, surfing and, of course, movie studios.

Doug Pfeiffer
VP Emeritus, International Skiing History Association
Honored Member Canadian and USA Ski Halls of Fame
August 2012

Doug Pfeiffer emigrated from the Laurentian Mountain ski resorts of Quebec in 1950, coming first for the opening years of Squaw Valley, California, to apprentice with the great Emile Allais, creator of the direct parallel from the start method of learning to ski. Soon after, he moved to Southern California to run ski schools first at Kratka Ridge and then Moonridge and Snow Summit. He left the region in 1963 to direct the ski school at Loveland Basin in Colorado and to become the editor in chief of *Skiing* magazine. In 1976, he returned to Snow Summit, where he still hangs his skis.

PREFACE

For the purpose of this book, a lost ski area is any area, public or private, that was outfitted with at least one tow or lift that no longer exists or is no longer operating. Included are two unique areas that were never graced with a flake of natural snow: Sepp Benedikter's Pine Needle Ski Slope in North Hollywood and Ski Villa in Carbon Canyon. Both areas operated rope tows for skiers to practice their turns on pine needles or schuss down a slope carpeted with plastic tiles.

Geographically, all ski areas located between Los Angeles and San Diego are included. With the exception of the Pine Needle Ski Slope and Ski Villa, all others were located in the Angeles National Forest, San Bernardino National Forest, San Jacinto Mountains or Cuyamaca Mountains.

ACKNOWLEDGEMENTS

All photographs and illustrations, unless otherwise noted, are in the author's collection housed in the California Ski Library. Many of these photographs are due to the generosity of a number of Southern California skiers and their families. My utmost thanks to:

Craig Van Degrift, son of Ethel Van Degrift, for his mother's incomparable archive.

Aileen Spiller, for Cecil Charles's photograph collection.

Claudia Benedikter Pedersen, for Sepp Benedikter's archive.

Jamie Lewis, daughter of Elmar Baxter, for her father's photograph collection.

Posthumously to Wolfgang Lert for his extensive photographic archive.

A number of other individuals made valuable contributions to the rich history of Southern California's lost ski areas:

Many thanks to Aubrie Koenig, commissioning editor at The History Press, for her guidance and suggestions throughout the development of this book.

Special thanks to Bev Brown, owner with husband Kerry of Rim Nordic Ski Area, and longtime mountain resident. Bev knows everyone and is an invaluable resource for tracking down people, information and photographs.

Thank you to Peter Brueggeman for his assistance with the history of Palomar Mountain Ski Area.

Ray Ransom generously provided photographs of the installation of Snow Forest's triple chairlift in 1981–82.

Thank you to Randy Pattison, former owner of Trinity Mountain Resort in Green Valley Lake, for insight into his personal history of the area.

Thank you to Carol Meyers of the San Diego History Center for help locating and access to photographs of Palomar Mountain Ski Area.

A special thank-you to Chuck Morse for his archive of Ski Villa memorabilia.

Thank you to Russ Keller, Lake Arrowhead historian, for access to his photograph collection and use of Green Valley Lake Snow Bowl photographs.

Thanks to Rick Metcalf for providing key information about Kratka Ridge since his purchase of the area.

Special thanks to Tom Preston for details about his family's O'Ongo Ski Tows.

Heartfelt thanks to longtime Wrightwood resident and historian Barbara Van Houten. She is an invaluable resource for all things Wrightwood and Big Pines.

Thanks to Douglas H. Milburn, U.S. Forest Service archaeologist for the Angeles National Forest, for his assistance with the early history of Table Mountain.

Many thanks to Karen Wullich Herbst for use of her historic San Diego Ski Club photographs and information about her mother, Dorothy McClung Wullich, first female member of the National Ski Patrol.

Thank you to Ann Dormer Johnson, daughter of Harlow Dormer, for use of her rare and extraordinary Table Mountain photographs.

Thank you to Lena Zimmerschied, public affairs manager for the Palm Springs Aerial Tramway, for help regarding the history of the rope tow at Mountain Station.

Thanks to Bob Smith of the Idyllwild Area Historical Society for photographs of Halona Hill.

I am indebted to Randy Thompson, senior archivist at the National Archives at Riverside, and his staff for their invaluable help accessing the San Bernardino National Forest archives.

Special thanks to Peg Wubben Weiler for access to her Uncle Bob Wubben's photographs of his historic Green Valley Lake ski tows.

I am indebted to Ray Hensley and the rest of the Hensley family for sharing their amazing thirty-three-year involvement in the history of Kratka Ridge. Thank you for the special meeting with the entire Hensley family and for access to the Hensley family Kratka Ridge archive.

Special thanks to Jill Salm Walker, daughter of Les Salm, for access to his remarkable Forest Service photo albums and Lake Arrowhead fire service daybooks. These lent many important new historical facts to Southern California ski history.

Last, a most special thank-you to ski historian extraordinaire and fellow ski book collector Doug Pfeiffer. From the beginning of work on my first book in 1999, Doug has been a most kind and generous mentor, always willing to provide suggestions, ideas, encouragement and humor. More importantly, I count him as a dear friend. Thanks, Doug.

INTRODUCTION

Since the turn of the twentieth century, the winter sports-minded residents of the Golden State have endured the long-held belief that it doesn't snow in California, especially Southern California. This was due in large part to the extraordinary marketing of the "sunshine" state by the California State Chamber of Commerce.

The realization that Southern California could become a winter sports mecca did not come easily. After many years of publicity highlighting seemingly eternal sunshine and year-round beaches, it would prove difficult to educate residents and tourists that California, especially the southern half, could accommodate winter sports as well as lay claim to perennial Mediterranean temperatures.

But things began to change in the late 1920s. The State Chamber of Commerce slowly realized that the state's once-taboo "white gold" could be a financial boon to more than just ski tow operators. It brought jobs to local communities. Businesses that were normally shuttered during the winter months could now cater to skiers and reap the monetary benefits that snow sports devotees brought to restaurants, lodges, gas stations and related businesses. Snow sports publicity and clear roads permanently changed the complexion of winter in California's snow-clad mountains.

The 1928 booklet *Los Angeles County Sport Land*, published by the Los Angeles Chamber of Commerce, described Southern California's unique geography: "When the Great White Blanket settles down on mountain slopes and lakes, they rival the Swiss Alps in scenic splendor. The view of fertile green valleys basking in the warm sunshine below those snow-covered peaks is an amazing sight. Some find it almost unbelievable that there could be such a great difference in so short a distance."

In 1929, the California State Chamber of Commerce began a statewide movement to "arouse the people to a realization of the magnificent natural attractions of the High Sierra in winter, and the opportunities for development of winter sports on a scale rivaling the famous winter playgrounds of Europe." In 1932, the chamber claimed, "California, the land of winter flowers and sunshine, bids fair to also become known the world over as 'The Land of the Ski.'"[1]

The publicity paid off, and skiing grew exponentially. The chamber began to track skier visits and estimated that 431,170 people visited California winter sports areas during the 1930–31 season. That number ballooned to 1,044,890 for the 1931–32 season, and it was estimated that 456,886 of those visits were to Southern California areas.[2]

However, a large number of those visitors attended winter carnivals to watch the thrills and derring-do of the mostly Scandinavian ski jumpers. At that time in Southern California, ski jumping was the most popular form of the sport, an event that was wildly popular with spectators. It was not a sport that most were willing to risk life and limb to try, but the winter carnivals and their ski jumping meets often garnered front-page headlines in Los Angeles newspapers. The liberal media exposure that ski jumping received aroused Southlanders out of their sun-drenched daze and awakened them to the winter sports possibilities in Southern California's mountains.

A 1937 *New York Times* article described the state of the winter sports scene in Southern California:

> *The high ranges around the orange-filled valleys are snow-clad every Winter and they have been made accessible over a modern system of mountain highways. As fine ski jumps and toboggan slides as may be found anywhere in America are now to be had within sixty to a hundred miles of where the more ambitious take January morning dives into the Pacific Ocean.*
>
> *Winter sports in Southern California have been followed by a few enthusiasts. Now, the universal American craze for skis has turned the California contingent into thousands.*[3]

Gradually, it was recognized that the future of skiing was the downhill variety. In the late 1930s, the Winter Sports Committee of the California State Chamber of Commerce reported, "As skiing is a downhill sport, ski tows are essential for the further development of skiing. California has been far behind in this development due to lack of interest on the part of private capital. Four ski tows were in operation last year: a rope tow at Donner Summit, a sled type tow in Yosemite, a sled type tow at the Auburn Ski Club, and a J-Bar type at Cold Springs."[4] Ten new tows were projected for the upcoming season.

Van Degrift's Ski Hut in Los Angeles became Southern California's first ski shop when it began to sell ski equipment in 1931. In 1934, Walter Mosauer, a zoology professor at the University of California–Los Angeles, considered the father of skiing here and an avid proponent of the Arlberg technique, wrote the first instructional ski book to be published in Southern California, *On Skis Over Mountains*. Mosauer, along with fellow German Otto Steiner, began teaching downhill skiing techniques, launching a change in focus and transition from ski jumping to alpine skiing.

Ethel Van Degrift, longtime ski writer for the *Los Angeles Times*, visited Aspen, Sun Valley, Mount Baker, Mount Hood and Mount Rainier in 1938. She drew an interesting comparison between those areas and Southern California areas. Still trying to buck the long-held belief that endless sunshine dominated year round, she acknowledged the advantages of Southern California's climate when taken together with skiing in the local mountain ranges. She commented:

> *We have several advantages which we don't quite appreciate until we ski in other parts of the country. One—is our almost unfailing sunshine, which adds much to the pleasure of skiing. Another is the proximity of ski areas to the cities. Still another—and really the most novel—is the fact that we may drive through sub-tropical countryside, among flowers and orange groves, to our skifields. This makes it easy to go skiing, when you compare it to those many places where one must drive fifty or a hundred miles through snow.*[5]

On weekends when winter carnivals were taking place, San Bernardino, Riverside and Redlands were crowded with visitors. Between January 25 and February 9, 1930, three winter carnivals took place in Southern California's mountains. Attendance at these carnivals was 52,500, and it was estimated that cities and towns en route reaped $100,000 from carnival goers.[6]

In the late 1930s and early 1940s, rope tows and other mechanical lifts began to sprout up in popular winter sports areas. In 1938 and 1939, Southern California's first mechanical tows were built at Big Bear Lake, Lake Arrowhead, Snow Valley, Table Mountain and other mountain communities. The outbreak of World War II put a virtual stop to most ski activity. But once the war was over and the state began to recover, skiing participation and ski area development began in earnest. Many of the Tenth Mountain Division servicemen returned to their home turf and began to develop areas or teach skiing to civilians. Ski tows and lifts removed the drudgery of uphill climbing. Skiing now appealed to the masses more than ever, and many flocked to the mountains on winter weekends.

After the completion of the Lynn Lift (a single chair) in 1949, Big Bear Lake could lay claim to having the greatest number of ski tows and lifts of any area in the United States. In the December 1949 issue of *The Skier*, the official publication of the Far West Ski Association, Frank Elkins wrote that Catamount in Massachusetts had eleven rope tows, making it "the greatest number of any area in the world."[7] Ralph Rupert, president of the Big Bear Winter Club, was quick to point out that with the recent completion of the Lynn Lift, Big Bear Valley had twelve.

Los Angeles Times ski writer Lynn Rogers gave an apt description of the mid-1950s ski boom in Southern California:

> *Southern California, Snow Sports Capital of the World! If our population keeps increasing and interest in winter sports continues at the present level you'll soon be reading this headline in newspapers and advertisements throughout the nation. For the past month with a white mantle of ermine covering the higher portions of the San Gabriel and San Bernardino Mountains thousands upon thousands of enthusiasts have been skiing, sledding, tobogganing, skating and frolicking in our great winter wonderland.*
>
> *So sunny Southern California with its tropical palm trees and white-sand beaches is gaining new fame. Brand new facilities for skiers have been completed atop many Southland mountain peaks and more are contemplated. New areas are open to outdoor lovers who are taking to snow sports in a big way.*[8]

In 1946, Southern California had one chairlift, the single chair at Mount Waterman. Ten years later, the Southland laid claim to fourteen ski areas outfitted with thirteen chairlifts, sixty-four rope tows and three Poma lifts within a one- to three-hour drive of Los Angeles.

Many of the small rope tow areas died out, but those that survived grew into some of Southern California's most popular areas, and these areas still thrive today: Snow Summit, Snow Valley, Mountain High and Bear Mountain. These areas had the financial ability, as well as the good fortune to have the water available to install extensive snow-making systems. The areas that did not have the capital or the water for snow making have either closed or remain operating at the mercy of Mother Nature. For example, during the 2001–2 season, Mount Waterman was closed due to lack of snow. In contrast, Mountain High was open for 150 days.[9] Formerly popular Southern California areas—Kratka Ridge, Ski Sunrise, Ski Green Valley, Snow Forest, Rebel Ridge and others—now exist only as memories in people's minds or scrapbooks. This book is the story of those lost areas, all of which played a part in the geographically challenged history that is Southern California skiing.

Chapter 1
LAKE ARROWHEAD TO RUNNING SPRINGS

The 1930s were halcyon years for skiing at Lake Arrowhead in the San Bernardino National Forest north of San Bernardino. Skiing flourished on the slopes around the village, and it was one of the first and favorite destinations for Southern California skiers. The Los Angeles Junior Chamber of Commerce, a dynamic force in the promotion of winter sports in the 1930s, chose Lake Arrowhead for its first winter carnival in 1927. A ski jump was built at Lake Arrowhead in 1932 and was often the central focus of the headline-attracting ski meets and winter carnivals, drawing ski jumpers from all over the nation.

Two of Southern California's pioneer ski mountaineers and ski instructors frequented the slopes of Lake Arrowhead and directed ski schools and winter sports programs there. First was Walter Mosauer, recruited by the North Shore Tavern to "reveal the mysteries of intricate Christianias, Telemarks and Tempo Turns."[10] Though it was advertised as a North Shore Tavern program, Mosauer's ski school took place at Keller Peak near Snow Valley, where an abundance of ski terrain, situated above six thousand feet, was often blanketed with more plentiful snow than the hills near the village at Lake Arrowhead. Later in the 1930s, Otto Steiner worked as director of the Lake Arrowhead Ski School. Much of Steiner's winter program also took place at Keller Peak.[11]

But all of these activities occurred without the luxury of mechanical uphill transportation. Edi Jaun and John Elvrum teamed up and built Lake Arrowhead's first mechanical tow in 1938. The sling lift, situated on a hill next to the Lake Arrowhead village school (where the fire station stands today), was easily accessible to guests staying at the Village Inn or any other local lodges. The 1,200-foot tow provided access to a wide choice of runs, from novice to

A 1930s map showing winter sports facilities for Lake Arrowhead winter visitors. The Lake Arrowhead North Shore Ski House, located at Fish Camp, was renamed Snow Valley in 1937. Note the emphasis on clear winter roads. Lack of access to ski areas was an obstacle for Southern California skiers prior to the advent of effective snow removal methods.

Edi Jaun (kneeling, far left) and John Elvrum (kneeling, third from left) teamed up to build Lake Arrowhead's first ski tow, a sling lift, in 1938. Upon his arrival in 1921, Jaun was one of Lake Arrowhead's first skiers. In addition to the Lake Arrowhead tow, he was also involved in the construction of the sling lift at Big Bear Lake. Elvrum, a championship ski jumper, went on to develop Snow Valley and owned and operated the area for more than thirty years.

expert. When snow conditions were favorable, the pair would use the lift to teach resort guests and locals. The two men were very active in promoting skiing opportunities and instruction to mountain residents.

Unfortunately, three low-snow years followed the construction of the tow, and it often sat idle. Tony Crowder bought the tow in the 1940s, but he, too, had limited success with the area. The snow season was often short and unpredictable, the low elevation of 5,174 feet frequently resulting in rain rather than snow.

Born on February 23, 1901, in Bern, Switzerland, Jaun and his family settled in Scranton, Pennsylvania, when he was six months old. For reasons unknown, he returned to Switzerland when he was six years of age and remained there for the next thirteen years. He climbed and skied all over Switzerland, firmly establishing his love of the mountains and skiing. In 1920, Jaun returned to the United States to live with an uncle in Pennsylvania.

Jaun's uncle learned that Lake Arrowhead village was being developed by J.B. Van Nuys and managed by Paul Bauman, a Swiss engineer. In 1921, Jaun came to Lake Arrowhead to look for work. By 1923, he owned the south shore marinas on the lake. He and his nephew Wilmer owned and operated the marina until it was sold in 1960.

Much of the early skiing that Jaun did around Lake Arrowhead was more for necessity than for sport. Since he was the only person working for the Lake Arrowhead Corporation who knew how to ski, he was often chosen to do winter repairs on downed telephone lines and carry mail on skis from the main highway to Lake Arrowhead. This trek was twenty-five miles round trip, and for two years, Jaun carried the mail once a week during winter when necessary.

Jaun and his wife, Eli, were expert cross-country skiers and ski jumpers. Edi competed in local races and won the five-mile cross-country race during the Seventh Annual Winter Sports Carnival held at Lake Arrowhead in 1933. He finished with a time of thirty-nine minutes, forty seconds. Eli competed in various cross-country races throughout the state and was often referred to as a star woman racer representing the Lake Arrowhead Ski Club. The two were also accomplished ski mountaineers. In 1934, along with five others, they scaled the summit of San Gorgonio on skis. After camping at the 6,000-foot level on Saturday night, the group started their ascent Sunday before dawn. Traveling by moonlight, they reached the 11,503-foot summit at 10:00 a.m. The others in the group were Walter Mosauer; Frederick C. Ripley Jr., president of the California Ski Association; Cliff Youngquist; Louis Turner; and Chet Allen.[12]

Edi is not known for his jumping, but in January 1934, a number of national newspapers featured a photograph of Halvor Halstad and Edi practicing a double jump that was to be featured during the upcoming California State Ski Championships.

Eli was one of less than a handful of female jumpers in the United States in the 1930s. In the December 1934 Utah Ski Club tournament, Edi competed in the A-class jumps, and Eli was the only woman who signed on for the "feminine class."[13]

Winter carnivals and ski jumping dominated the 1930s winter sports scene, but these activities were severely limited or came to a standstill once World War II broke out. But when the war ended in 1945, there was great interest in reviving the popularity of Lake Arrowhead and other Southern California winter sports centers to levels equal or above those experienced in the 1930s.

Les Salm, Lake Arrowhead's first fire chief, was active in establishing postwar skiing at Lake Arrowhead.[14] Salm went to work for the Lake Arrowhead

The Lodge Hill Ski Tow, a rope tow Les Salm built in Lake Arrowhead in the 1940s, was the beneficiary of his snow-making experiments in 1947–48. Snowfall at Lake Arrowhead was often marginal, prompting Salm to begin experimenting with snow making in 1947. Salm's young son David pauses for a break on a slope blanketed with man-made snow. *Courtesy of Jill Salm Walker.*

This skier has discovered a unique way to rest as he ascends the Lodge Hill Ski Tow. *Courtesy of Jill Salm Walker.*

County Fire District on July 20, 1942. He had been a San Bernardino National Forest ranger since 1926–27 and spent many of his fourteen years with the Forest Service patrolling on motorcycle. He built a rope tow in Lake Arrowhead (the exact date of construction is unknown) and dubbed it the Lodge Hill Ski Tow. It was operating in the mid- to late 1940s and was one of the locations where Salm conducted early experiments with snow making. In Salm's daybooks from 1947–48, there is no mention of this ski tow, but he does provide an outline of his historic attempts at making snow.

The first successful snow making at a ski area in the United States was at Walter Schoenknecht's Mohawk Mountain Ski Area in Cornwall, Connecticut, in 1950–51. In 1955, Moonridge Meadows, now Big Bear's Bear Mountain Ski Area, was the first California ski area to successfully implement snow making. Salm's approach was different from others who attempted to manufacture snow. Snow making then and now employs a system of hoses and nozzles. Salm's method was cloud seeding.

Salm may have been inspired by work that had taken place at General Electric in Schenectady, New York. In November 1946, Dr. Bernard Vonnegut discovered that microscopic silver iodide crystals acted as a nucleus for water vapor to form ice crystals. General Electric rented an airplane and released dry ice into the clouds on four days in November and December 1946. On the last day of the seeding, the greatest snowfall of the winter blanketed Schenectady. It is likely that Salm learned of this work and felt it could be the answer to Lake Arrowhead's often marginal snowfall. In early November 1947, Salm consulted with Big Bear Lake's Clifford Lynn and the Lake Arrowhead Chamber of Commerce about snow making. He then went forward with his experiments and documented these activities in his daybooks. Below are his narratives of his snow-making attempts during the 1947–48 season:

> *November 14, 1947—Made preparations to precipitate snow or rain with dry ice and balloon. Temperatures did not drop low enough.*
>
> *November 15, 1947—Cold north wind blew rain clouds away. Snowed at Big Bear and fog iced the trees. Clouds too warm here to send up dry ice balloons.*
>
> *November 20, 1947—Received hydrogen and dry ice for snowmaking.*
>
> *November 22, 1947—Snowed 1½ inches between 4am and 8am from putting dry ice in the clouds at S.P.L.O.* [Strawberry Peak Lookout]. *Sent six hydrogen balloons with dry ice into clouds and it snowed from 9am to 2pm.*
>
> *December 3, 1947—At 2pm I released 2 balloons with dry ice from Summit. Nothing happened. Cloud was too warm. About 4:20pm Rusty Wiles and I flew dry ice with a box kit into clouds from Strawberry Peak Lookout. In about 10 minutes it began to snow on the Peak and rain fell at Blue Jay, Alpine, and Lake Arrowhead. After snowing for 20 minutes, the kit broke away and it stopped snowing almost immediately, but rain continued to fall at lower elevations.*
>
> *January 25, 1948—Moist marine air swept into Southern California today…This is the first moisture in 7 weeks of droughth* [sic]. *I tried to get dry ice to fly into the fog with box kit to start precipitation.*
>
> *February 4, 1948—9pm went to Crest Summit and attempted to fly dry ice into clouds but wind was too gusty to launch kite.*

Salm's snow-making experiments were the first attempts to manufacture snow for skiing in California and some of the earliest in the United States.

In February 1947, the season before Salm began his snow-making efforts, Walt and Wynne Harmon advertised "California's new winter sports center" with the opening of a two-thousand-foot sling lift and rope tows at Lake Arrowhead. They experienced the frustration that marginal snowfall could inflict on Southern California ski area operators, and the lifts ran intermittently.

The last attempt at developing a successful Lake Arrowhead ski enterprise took place during the 1961–62 season. The Lake Arrowhead Ski Bowl opened with a double rope tow. In the event of no natural snow, it was reported that artificial snow "will be cut and spread a fresh two inches deep across the bowl each night after December 15 [1961]."[15]

In addition to the various Lake Arrowhead tows, other lifts sprang up along slopes from Lake Arrowhead to Running Springs. Cedar Glen, nestled into the trees at the east end of Lake Arrowhead, began as a lumber operation. In 1916, lumberman John Suverkrup subdivided fifty-six lots and named it Cedar Glen. As the homesites developed and the town grew in popularity, the need for a business district at the east end of the lake arose. Suverkrup then developed a small grocery store and rental cabins.

By the late 1940s, Cedar Glen was a destination for all manner of winter sports enthusiasts. Visitors could take in a sleigh ride from the O.P. Doan stables located at the entrance to the town.

A January 1947 advertisement for Walt and Wynne Harmon's Lake Arrowhead ski area. They spared no expense outfitting the area with the latest in ski rentals, clothing and accessories, but winter weather was fickle, and the area was short-lived due to inadequate snowfall.

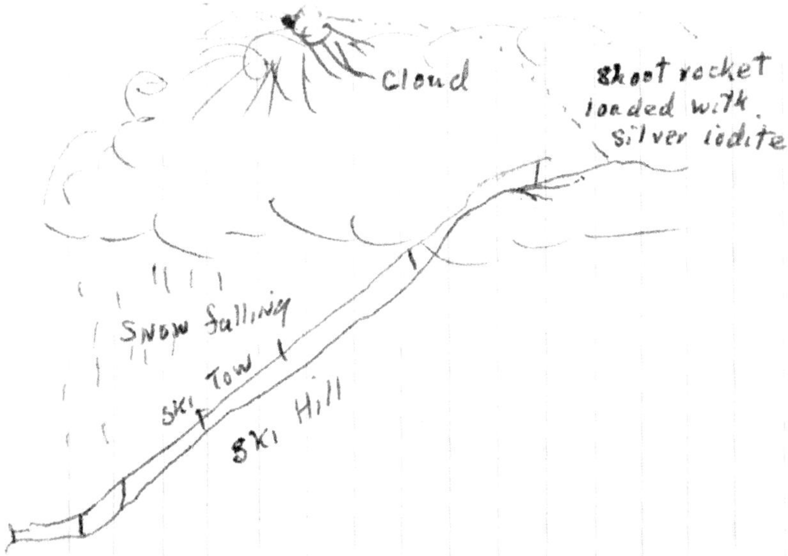

A hand-drawn sketch from Les Salm's October 1947 fire service daybook illustrating his plan to produce man-made snow on his Lake Arrowhead ski hill. His snow-making attempts, for the specific purpose of augmenting the snowpack for skiing, were the first in California. *Courtesy of Jill Salm Walker.*

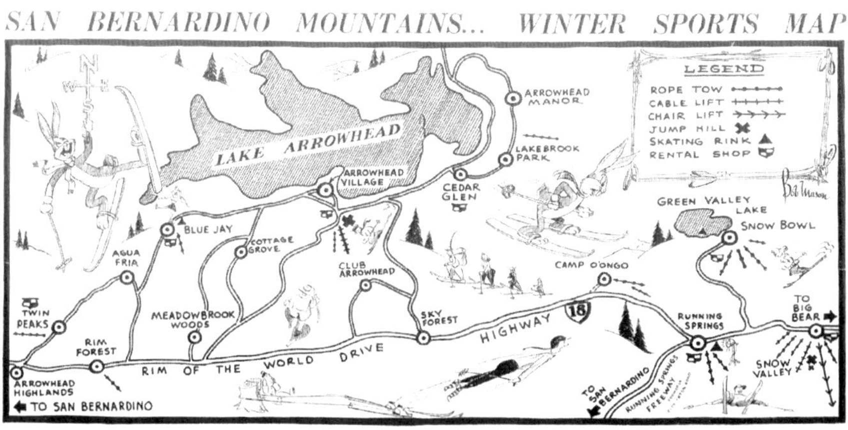

A whimsical 1949 winter sports map showing the location of the many ski tows that sprang up between Twin Peaks and Snow Valley.

SKI TOW

OPERATING ON OPEN ROAD

WRITE—
Cedar Glen Co. Cedar Glen, Calif.

For Information Phone
Lake Arrowhead 8122

A no-frills 1949 advertisement for Cedar Glen's rope tow.

Beyond Cedar Glen, at the foot of Hook hill on the county highway, skiers could ride the one-thousand-foot-long ski tow that operated throughout the winter season. Ski instructors were available for those wanting to polish their skills or for novices just learning the fundamentals. For non-skiers, toboggan runs and sledding hills were on hand.

Blue Jay, a quaint community located approximately one mile from Lake Arrowhead Village, operated a rope tow from 1948 through 1959. The tow, 500 feet long with a 150-foot rise, ran whenever snow conditions allowed. At an elevation of 5,203 feet, the slope often suffered from marginal snowfall.

Tom Preston founded and operated O-Ongo Ski Tows. Located two and a half miles west of Running Springs on Highway 18 at an elevation of 6,400 feet, the area opened during the 1945–46 season and, by the mid-1950s, operated five rope tows providing access to slopes for all levels of skiers. The area closed in 1957, another victim of low elevation and unpredictable snowfall.

Howard Martin ran a one-thousand-foot tow just outside Running Springs in the 1940s. In 1947, Martin left Running Springs and became the manager

BLUE JAY *Resort*

ADJOINING LAKE ARROWHEAD
OPEN ALL YEAR

BLUE JAY, CALIFORNIA

WINTER SPORTS

- ICE SKATING
- SKIING
- SKI TOW
- SLEDDING
- TOBOGGANING
- SKI SHOP
- SKI EQUIPMENT FOR SALE OR RENT

ACCOMMODATIONS

- FURNISHED CABINS
- HOTEL ROOMS

STORES & SHOPS

- COFFEE SHOP
- COCKTAIL LOUNGE
- DRUG STORE
- FOOD MARKET
- HOME BAKERY
- SERVICE STATION
- OTHER STORES, SHOPS & AMUSEMENT

STOP & SHOP — STAY & PLAY at BLUE JAY

Ample FREE parking. A complete Resort & Village for the year 'round vacationeer.

For further information and reservations write BLUE JAY RESORT, Blue Jay, Cal.

Blue Jay has facilities and accommodations which enables this resort community to operate the year 'round and provides both a complete shopping and amusement center.

★ ★ ★

The Ice Skating Rink is open from Christmas Day until about April 1st. It re-opens again on Memorial Day and remains open for the Summer Season until October 1st each year.

★ ★ ★

During the winter months there is a Ski Tow with an excellent hill for the novice and family group. For the non-skiier, there are nearby hills where sledding and tobogganing may be enjoyed. Winter Sports equipment may be rented or purchased at the Ski Shop and a general repair service is maintained by Walter D. Heidman, who also builds Skis' to order.

★ ★ ★

Excellent cabin and hotel accommodations may be had by the day or week at very modest rates throughout the year.

★ ★ ★

Blue Jay invites you for Winter, Spring, Summer and Fall.

Blue Jay, a small community adjacent to Lake Arrowhead, was often overshadowed by the more popular Lake Arrowhead. In the 1950s, Blue Jay also began providing a variety of ski facilities, including a rope tow, to entice winter sports enthusiasts to visit the small town.

of the ski tows at Conway Summit near Bridgeport in the Eastern Sierra Nevada. Lloyd Soutar also operated a tow in Running Springs. In the mid-1950s, he installed an eight-hundred-foot tow, mostly for his family to use, immediately west of the current elementary school.

A 1949 advertisement for Camp O'Ongo's Ski Hill highlighting facilities and amenities that catered to skiers.

Beginning in the 1949–50 season, two rope tows, both 750 feet long with a 175-foot rise, operated in Running Springs. It is unknown who operated these tows, but Bob Mason provided ski instruction. They operated through the mid-1950s, and then, beginning with the 1955–56 season, this area became known as Wintergarten. The tows continued to operate until sometime in the 1960s.

In January 1965, Ski the Rim opened on Rim of the World Highway in Running Springs. One 600-foot rope tow with a 250-foot vertical rise operated on the four-acre hill. Its elevation often resulted in marginal snowfall, so owner Bob French designed his own snow-making equipment purported to make snow at thirty-eight degrees, nine degrees higher than traditional snow-making systems.

Ski the Rim was outfitted for night skiing, with ski lessons available under the lights. As with many of the other nearby ski facilities, Ski the Rim had a variety of shortcomings. In addition to uncertain snowfall, the area lacked a paved entrance road and did not have a large enough warming hut.

Over the years, enthusiasm for winter sports ran high in Lake Arrowhead, and it was one of the foremost destinations for Southern California ski enthusiasts. But at an elevation of approximately 5,100 feet, its ski slopes were often showered with raindrops rather than snowflakes. Eventually, skiers knew they could count on snow at higher elevations near Snow Valley or a number of Big Bear Lake areas, leaving Lake Arrowhead devoid of winter sports facilities.

Chapter 2

Green Valley Lake

Green Valley Lake, a small community located five miles east of Running Springs and approximately thirty miles from San Bernardino, first became a winter sports area in the 1920s. In 1925, Los Angeles developers DeWitt and Blair began building roads and subdividing lots. When the dam was completed in 1926, a widespread advertising campaign was launched. DeWitt and Blair built a clubhouse and started what they called the Top o' the World Club, whose membership was open to any Green Valley Lake lot owner. In February 1929, the Top o' the World Club began preparing a large area of the lake for ice skating, and the State Highway Department cleared Green Valley Lake Road in anticipation of the crowds that would make the trip to Green Valley Lake if ice skating was available. A toboggan slide had also been completed, and a hill for ski jumpers was in the planning stages.[16]

Before Green Valley Lake Snow Bowl was developed in 1945–46, some local residents installed their own rope tows for ski and toboggan runs. Les Salm, later to become Lake Arrowhead's first fire chief, pioneered this effort when he constructed Green Valley Lake's first tow in 1937. He installed a three-hundred-foot rope tow, powered by a seven-horsepower Briggs and Stratton engine. The tow was approximately 150 yards uphill, behind Joe and Eleanor Fox's Trading Post, at what is now known locally as Suicide Hill. Bob Wubben, a longtime resident of Green Valley Lake, designed and built the power assembly at the bottom of the hill. Fox's Trading Post provided food and served as a warming hut for the skiers. Wubben's wife Doris recalled, "The Trading Post became the funhouse of Green Valley."[17]

Salm, born in Michigan in 1908, made a number of contributions to Southern California's early ski history. He and his family came from Grand Rapids, Michigan, to the Torrance area in 1911. He became a San

Les Salm's Green Valley Lake rope tow, built in 1937, was one of Southern California's first ski tows. *Courtesy of Jill Salm Walker.*

Salm's hand-built tow motor for his Green Valley Lake ski tow, along with a sign advertising ten-cent tow rides. *Courtesy of Jill Salm Walker.*

Les Salm at Mill Creek Ranger Station, 1929. A skier from a young age, he built two of the first rope tows in Southern California, one at Fish Camp (Snow Valley) in 1932 and the other at Green Valley Lake in 1937. *Courtesy of Jill Salm Walker.*

Bernardino National Forest ranger in 1926–27 and, through his motorcycle patrols, became intimately acquainted with the forest from Lake Arrowhead to Snow Valley. He worked as a ranger until 1942, when he began working for the Lake Arrowhead County Fire District. He served as Lake Arrowhead's fire chief for twenty-three years. Not only did he construct Green Valley Lake's first tow, but he also later revitalized post–World War II skiing in Lake Arrowhead. He was also responsible for giving Snow Valley its name. In the early 1930s, the area was known as Fish Camp. By the latter half of the 1930s, it had become extremely popular with skiers and was a favorite destination of the Lake Arrowhead crowd. As a result, Salm began referring to the area as Snow Valley. At the end of 1937, with the encouragement and backing of Sverre Engen, who had been running the ski operation, the Forest Service formally changed the name to Snow Valley.

It is also possible that Salm built the first rope tow in California. In one of his historic 1930s photo albums, he recounted that, in 1922, the road ended at Fish Camp. The area was dotted with six cabins, and John Swetkovich, nicknamed Johnnie Sixbits, operated a sawmill there. Salm wrote that he built a one-thousand-foot-long rope tow, using Swetkovich's steam-powered logging donkey engine for power. He also noted that as many as ten people used the tow on some Sundays.

The 1922 date is likely incorrect, since Salm would have been about fourteen years old. It is apparent that he meant to write "1932," which is when Salm was an active Forest Service ranger and would have frequently been patrolling the Fish Camp area. The 1932 date is nevertheless significant because, with the exception of Truckee's 1910 toboggan tow that skiers adopted as a ski lift, Salm's Fish Camp tow was California's first rope tow.

Green Valley Lake's other pioneer rope tow builder was Bob Wubben. During the 1940–41 season, he built a rope tow about 150 yards east of Salm's tow. His tow was powered by an old automobile engine mounted on a concrete base situated at the top of the run.[18] Both tows sat at the east end of Meadow Lane. When Green Valley Lake Snow Bowl opened in the winter of 1945–46, the equipment from the Suicide Hill tows was put to use there.

In 1950, Bob and Doris Wubben bought the original equipment back from Green Valley Lake Snow Bowl, obtained a lease from the Forest Service to operate at Suicide Hill and set up two toboggan runs. Wubben used Ford Model A wheels, mounted on trees at the top and bottom of the runs, as pulleys to guide the rope. The runs traveled five hundred feet down toward Green Valley Lake Road. Tobogganers would sometimes reach speeds of forty-five miles per hour. The runs had a starting gate to help keep the toboggans from sliding downhill before the riders were ready. The Wubbens awarded a prize

Bob Wubben, longtime Green Valley Lake resident and winter sports pioneer. He helped Les Salm build Green Valley Lake's first ski tow and later built his own tows for skiing and tobogganing. *Courtesy of Peg Wubben Weiler.*

to anyone who made it down the hill, across the creek and to the finish at Green Valley Lake Road. They later added a third run that traveled around the side of the hill and had banked S curves like a bobsled run. The high cost of liability insurance forced the closure of the operation in 1953.

On March 1, 1955, the Wubbens obtained a Forest Service permit to develop a small ski run on the back of their property on Green Valley Lake Road. They used the same Briggs and Stratton engine and other equipment from the toboggan runs. The tow was used by family members and guests. The Wubbens operated this tow until 1967.

Though little is left of Les Salm's and Bob Wubben's tows, and few remain who remember them, they were the first rope tows in the Green

View of the base area of Wubben's rope tow looking toward Green Valley Lake Road. Wubben operated the tow, built in 1955 behind his cabin, for use by family and friends. *Courtesy of Peg Wubben Weiler.*

Valley Lake area and provided family members and locals a place to gather for winter sports fun.

Larry Ferguson, Joe Fox and Ernest C. "Doc" Vawter founded Green Valley Lake Snow Bowl in the winter of 1945–46. They chose the slopes in Green Valley because of high snowfall amounts and the fact that snow clung to Green Valley Lake's north-facing slopes longer than most other Southern California mountain areas. Green Valley Lake Snow Bowl, with a base elevation of approximately seven thousand feet, was higher than any other San Bernardino Mountain ski resort.

The three founders established the Green Valley Lake Corporation on October 15, 1946. Joe Fox, president, managed the ski area in 1945 and 1946. He also operated a ski tow on private land. Vawter, vice-president, managed Hoyt Heater Company in Los Angeles and had been a property owner and resident of Green Valley Lake beginning in 1935. Ferguson, secretary-treasurer, and his wife moved to Green Valley Lake in 1938. Ferguson, a partner with Joe Fox in Fox Lumber, operated the clubhouse, real estate office and boat dock and was active in ski area operations from its beginnings in

Larry Ferguson, along with Joe Fox and Ernest C. "Doc" Vawter, founded Green Valley Lake Snow Bowl in 1945–46. Ferguson was active in the development and management of the area from its beginnings until his death in 1974. *Courtesy of Lyle Ferguson.*

1945 until his death in 1974. The men were involved with primarily summer businesses and wanted to develop a venture that would provide recreation for local residents, as well as revenue, during the winter months.

The Snow Bowl began with two rope tows, the 1,100-foot "Big Tow" and the 600-foot "Little Tow." In late 1947, the three partners made significant improvements to the area. They cleared and smoothed ski runs and filled gullies. A network of intersecting runs and open areas was designed to give skiers a greater variety of trails. That same year, construction was completed on a warming hut, which housed a snack bar, rental room and restroom.

Area improvements continued into 1948. Slopes were again bulldozed and cleared. Extensive work created new advanced runs in the upper bowl. A new ski school slope with its own tow was available free of charge to ski school students, and a new building dedicated for National Ski Patrol use was constructed from timber removed from the ski hill. Green Valley had a well-trained and organized ski patrol providing as many as eleven patrolmen on weekends.

A view of Green Valley Lake Snow Bowl's base area, outfitted with a day lodge and rope tow. Though the area was small, skiers could often find plentiful powder due to Green Valley Lake's north-facing slopes and seven-thousand-foot base elevation. *Courtesy of Russ Keller.*

Skiers ride the small tow at Green Valley Lake Snow Bowl. *Courtesy of Russ Keller.*

In the early 1950s, a number of new Southern California ski areas were born, and existing ski areas made improvements and installed chairlifts. In 1954, wanting to improve the lifts at the Snow Bowl, Ferguson traveled to Arapahoe Basin, Colorado, to examine a Poma lift. So, in addition to its three rope tows, the area became the first in Southern California to install a Poma lift. The 1,280-foot-long lift arrived from Europe by boat and was transported to Green Valley Lake on Fox's lumber truck. Ferguson's son Lyle recalled that the lift arrived just like a "TinkerToy kit."[19]

Green Valley Lake Snow Bowl was not a moneymaker for any of the three partners but continued to survive through good seasons and bad. Lyle Ferguson commented, "It was something that everybody felt was absolutely a part of their soul; the ski hill was the valley and the valley was the ski hill, as well as the lake. Being a part of that was really a wonderful experience…to grow up with that environment."[20]

The three founders continued to operate the area until 1960. Doc Vawter, who had essentially remained a silent partner, moved away from Green Valley Lake. Earl Voorhees, who had been involved in other ski areas, bought Vawter's share of the business. However, the deal did not result in a three-way split. Ferguson and Fox retained a controlling interest in the area. In contrast to Vawter, Voorhees was an active, hands-on partner. After he joined the duo, he expanded runs and improved terrain.

Around 1970, Joe and Eleanor Fox sold their lumberyard and wanted to sell their share in the ski area. So, in 1972, Don and Ann Howe, longtime Green Valley Lake skiers and ski patrol members, became partners in the Green Valley Lake Corporation. Ann Howe renamed the area Ski Green Valley, immediately making her mark on the area.

Another partnership change took place in 1974 when Larry Ferguson died. Lyle Ferguson assumed his father's position in the corporation. Lyle had been working at the ski area since he was twelve years old. After his father's death, his role did not change significantly since he had been heavily involved and worked at the area every year, only now he was an official partner in the enterprise.

Not long before Ferguson's death, Voorhees became less active in the business and decided he wanted to sell his share. Ferguson and the Howes bought Voorhees's share, and the area became a fifty-fifty partnership.

Ferguson and the Howes operated Ski Green Valley until 1986, when Lloyd and Catherine Peake purchased the area. The Peakes immediately made significant improvements: they purchased a new snowcat, remodeled the lodge and installed Ski Green Valley's first chairlift.

In 1993–94, with the burgeoning popularity of snowboarding, the Peakes renamed the resort Big Air Green Valley. In conjunction with the name change, the area became a snowboard-only resort. In January 1993, snowboarding-only began on a six- to eight-week trial basis, with the resort catering to snowboarders Monday through Friday. Skiers still had access to the resort on weekends and holidays.

Nationally, skier numbers had been dwindling while snowboarders were increasing steadily. Many ski areas had refused to allow snowboarders on their slopes. But as snowboarding entered the mainstream and ski areas realized the effect snowboarders could have on their bottom line, resorts began to cater to riders as well as skiers. Big Air Green Valley, at fifty acres the smallest of Southern California's ski resorts, was in a very difficult market, competing against Snow Valley, Bear Mountain and Snow Summit with their longer runs and greater number of lifts. Eric Schwarz, director of marketing at Big Air Green Valley, expressed the frustration the resort was experiencing at that time: "The writing is on the wall. In a zero-growth industry, this is the only thing that's growing. It's rough for the big guys [in the Southern California ski market]. We cannot compete with them, so we needed to find another way to stand out."[21]

In its inaugural season as Big Air Green Valley, the resort met with limited success due to lack of snow and a limited snow-making system. It was a risk to create the West's first snowboard-only park, and many longtime Ski Green

Valley devotees were unhappy with the change. After all, the area had been the quintessential mom and pop family ski resort whose clientele was mostly made up of Green Valley Lake cabin owners, other mountain residents and skiers who wanted to avoid the "carnival at Snow Valley and the mob scene at Big Bear."[22]

The area's ski runs were only half the length of those at Snow Valley, Snow Summit and Bear Mountain, but the area compensated by adding challenging obstacles. A number of man-made and natural jumps were created along with side rails installed throughout the area. There was also a half-pipe serviced by a rope tow.

By 1996, Peake had brought in Dave Wilson and eventually transferred the area to him. Big Air Green Valley continued to struggle financially, and in 1998, the resort changed its name to Big Air Winter Park, signaling the return of skiers to the area. However, in May 1999, Wilson asked Ferguson and the Howes to take the area back. The trio accepted and regained ownership, but within a few months, they made a deal with Calvary Chapel, owners of a nearby summer camp, to manage and operate the area.

Big Air Winter Park did not open during the 1999–2000 and 2000–1 seasons due to late-season snowfall and the uncertainty of ownership status. Under Calvary Chapel's management, the area operated only intermittently, and when Randy Pattison and Ron Bigelow took ownership in the fall of 2005, the resort had been sitting idle with the exception of a couple of weekends in February 2002.

Pattison renamed the area Trinity Mountain Resort. Calvary Chapel had planned to run the resort as part of its ministry, but the new owners planned to run the area as a business but with a Christian twist. Smoking, alcohol and offensive language were not permitted.

Pattison and Bigelow made much-needed improvements to the area, including remodeling the base lodge. The 2005–6 season started late; Trinity Mountain did not open until March but was able to remain open for thirty one days. In spring 2006, the pair began working on getting a snow-making system in place. Then, during the summer of 2006, Bigelow resigned as vice-president to pursue other interests. Pattison remained as president/CEO, and Craig Carlson served as chief financial officer. The owners had invested more than $250,000 to get the area up and running, but the 2006–7 season was dismal. They opened for only three days of skiing that season. Pattison explained the difficulties of area operations at that point:

> *Our frustration was for the 34 days we used the resort we were profitable on a daily basis. Snowmaking was to be our golden addition and key for success. One of the major issues we had when we took over the resort was erosion…*

> *We worked hard to keep the mountain out of Green Valley Lake. On February 28, 2006 we lost the erosion battle and during a 100 year flood the town of Green Valley Lake was covered with silt from our mountain. It was a massive cleanup effort.*[23]

Then, on October 22, 2007, the massive Slide Fire, pushed by severe Santa Ana winds, surrounded Green Valley Lake, destroying over one hundred homes, the ski hill's outbuildings and the area's only chairlift. Pattison recounted the grim circumstances:

> *The fire came in from the east and burned through the bottom motor room of the main chair. The lodge was spared thanks to a drop of retardant from a tanker. We parked the snow grooming machines in the middle of a ski run and the fire burned within 10 feet but caused no damage. The top of the main chairlift's counter weight that holds the tension on the cable melted, causing the lift to lose tension. Dismantling the chairlift was a major undertaking. Insurance coverage was not enough to handle a complete rebuild, so all we could do was surrender the permit back to the Forest Service and return the area back to its natural state.*[24]

Over the years, the Green Valley Lake Snow Bowl, in all its incarnations, provided what one journalist called a "rare luxury these days: a quiet day of relaxed and highly enjoyable low-voltage skiing."[25] Unfortunately, in its last years, Green Valley's ski area struggled through numerous ownership changes, lack of snow making and years of limited or no snowfall. The Slide Fire in 2007 was the death knell from which the resort could not recover.

Chapter 3

BIG BEAR LAKE

Sling Lift/Lynn Lift/Snow Forest

Big Bear's first ski tow, a sling lift, was built in 1938 and was one of three of the nation's first overhead cable lifts.[26] Most winter sports locations around the country, if they had any mechanical lift at all, had rope tows. Rope tows were difficult and tiring to use, prompting a variety of other designs and methods for uphill transportation. The unique overhead cables took the place of waist-height ropes.

Judge Clifford Lynn, who is most well known for his role in the construction of Big Bear Lake's first chairlift in 1949, was also responsible for the creation of the sling lift. Lynn was well acquainted with Big Bear winters. In March 1913, while a caretaker at Pine Knot, he snowshoed out of Bear Valley after three feet of new snow had fallen over sixteen hours.[27] He went on to found the Big Bear Lake Park District in 1934, signaling the beginning of organized winter sports promotion for Big Bear Valley.

Prior to the construction of the sling lift, ski jumping reigned as the king of winter sports in Big Bear Lake and throughout Southern California mountains. In fact, the first Special Use Permit that Lynn applied for and received on December 22, 1937, was to "construct and maintain a ski jump."[28] But Lynn and Tommi Tyndall, founder and developer of Snow Summit, would later be most influential in guiding Big Bear Valley from the ski jumping era to the alpine era.

Less than a year after receiving the Special Use Permit for a ski jump, Lynn applied for a second Special Use Permit on October 6, 1938. This permit included construction of a ski tow, ski hut, chemical toilet and power plant shed. It was approved on November 2, 1938, and work on the tow began immediately. Lake Arrowhead ski pioneer Edi Jaun erected the towers for the 1,200-foot sling lift.[29] The *Mountaineer* reported that the location would be "one of the finest ski fields in the mountains," but the Big Bear Lake Park District was still formulating a plan to get skiers from the center of town to the area.[30] If the road to the area proved too difficult, skiers could be transported from Pine Knot and Big Bear Boulevard in Sid Sutherland's weasel.

Donald Dawson designed the Big Bear sling lift, a jig-back affair, and fashioned it after the Fish Camp (Snow Valley) tow, also built in 1938. The sling lift carried a series of ten slings on each side ending in triangular grips hanging from an overhead cable suspended about ten feet off the ground. In spite of stationary loading, boarding the tow was cumbersome.

Skiers waited in line at the bottom of the hill, standing next to two rows of twelve stakes each. When the empty slings came to a stop, one sling sat next to each stake. Once the slings were in place, the skiers stepped into position and hooked their ski poles into little clips, grasped the triangular slings with both hands and waited. When all ten skiers were ready, the operator started the lift. The skiers were pulled uphill as long as they kept hanging onto the sling. Empty slings came down on the other side.

Big Bear Lake's sling lift, one of three built in Southern California. The others were at Lake Arrowhead and Fish Camp (Snow Valley). *Photo by Elmar Baxter.*

The lift moved along at three to four miles per hour. If someone fell, which was a common occurrence, the operator stopped the lift until the skier was on his feet. The lift then started again. When the skiers reached the top of the run, the lift stopped to let them unload. At the same time, skiers at the bottom of the hill were hooking up. The direction of the cable reversed, and the cycle repeated.

A tow ticket for Big Bear Lake's first ski tow, a sling lift. Clifford Lynn received the Special Use Permit in November 1938, and the tow began operating shortly thereafter. Skiers accustomed to strenuous uphill climbing to earn their downhill runs were more than happy to pay for an easy and fast ride to the top.

Dick Kun, chief executive officer of Big Bear Mountain Resorts, remembered riding the lift as a ten-year-old: "I hung on to that trapeze ring for dear life. Every time the grip on the haul-rope passed over a sheave on the tower I'd get hoisted a few feet off the ground."[31]

Lift capacity was 200 persons per hour;[32] 12 skiers were carried up the hill every two and a quarter minutes.[33] Some of today's lifts carry 3,600 skiers per hour, but skiers were more than happy to catch a ride on the old sling lift, a workhorse for more than twenty years. On one busy weekend in 1947, three thousand rides were sold.

Frank Moore, Redlands historian and former editor of the *Redlands Daily Facts*, gave a detailed description of the sling lift to the Sierra Club Ski Mountaineers:

> *The tow will be located about ⅛ mi. from the business center of Pine Knot. The altitude at the bottom is 7000', and the run is a dip profile, steeper at the top, 1070 feet long, with a rise of 225 ft. The time for a trip from bottom to top is estimated to be 1⅛ minutes. No definite charge for tow rides has been set; built by the Big Bear Park Dist. from public monies, it will be*

> *operated on a non-profit basis. Technicalities of possible interest to Up-Ski Engineers are: there are 8 steel towers set in concrete, 14ft. high and 8-ft. crossarms; 10" ball bearing sheaves and 9/16" -6 strand plow steel cable. Power is furnished by a Ford V8 motor.*[34]

From these modest beginnings, Big Bear Lake eventually grew from a summer-only resort to the winter sports capital of Southern California. In the mid-1940s, the *Grizzly* reported, "Big Bear has long been the vacation mecca for thousands of Southern Californians who enjoy mountain outings and lake fishing and water sports; but more and more the valley is coming into its own as a winterland of vacation thrills."[35] But as late as 1947, Big Bear was described as "really a summer resort, with only a few of the motels and hotels bothering to stay open during the winter. Season is January through March. Only upski of any importance is behind the town of Big Bear itself, and is a compensating saddle type lift like Snow Valley's. Bill Munson operates a rope tow at Bear City, just a few miles beyond Big Bear Lake higher in the mountains."[36]

However, it was also in 1947 that the community of Big Bear finally began to equip itself for its role as the winter sports capital of Southern California. The Winter Sports Committee of the Big Bear Lake Chamber of Commerce attempted to secure a certified instructor from the California Ski Association. The committee also began to campaign actively to attract intercollegiate ski teams and clubs in the California Ski Association to hold their meets in Big Bear Valley.

Coincidentally, Tommi Tyndall, founder of Snow Summit in 1952, came to Big Bear Lake in 1947–48. The Chamber of Commerce needed to look no further for an instructor. Tyndall arrived in Big Bear already experienced in ski instruction and ski school development. He taught in Sun Valley's ski school and had started ski schools at Cannon Mountain, New Hampshire, and Wilmot Hills, Wisconsin. He established ski schools at the sling lift and the Lynn chairlift, which he used as his center of operations. He founded the Big Bear Winter Club, which held its first Snow Carnival in 1949. He consolidated his Big Bear Lake ski schools in 1948 and ran them under the name Mill Creek Ski Schools. In January 1949, he changed the name to Big Bear Certified Ski School. In addition to the Lynn Lift, the ski schools operated at the Mill Creek Ski Bowls, Moonridge, the Sugar Loaf area and the Swiss Ski Tow.[37]

Big Bear Lake's first chairlift, the Lynn Lift, was built in 1949. The only other chairlifts operating in Southern California at this time were the Mount Waterman chair, built in 1942; the Blue Ridge chairlift, built in 1947; and the recently completed chairlift at Snow Valley. All four were single chairs.

Judge Lynn, former chairman of the Big Bear Lake Park District, was the moving force behind the lift. The three-thousand-foot chair was located near the sling lift area on the slopes a few hundred yards south of the village. It had sixty chairs and a seven-hundred-foot rise. The ride took about ten minutes, and 240 skiers could be whisked to the top of the hill every hour.

Lynn worked tirelessly to bring about the completion of the chairlift. He originally submitted the application for construction of the lift in September 1940, and it was approved by the Forest Service on October 7, 1940. Had construction gone forward at this time, it would have been Southern California's first chairlift. A cumulative tax fund had been set aside to finance the project.

Also in September 1940, Lynn submitted two different sets of chairlift plans to the Forest Service. Hoping to expedite approval and the bid process, one of the plans he submitted was for a chairlift similar in design to one that had already been approved by the Forest Service in Bishop. He expressed a desire to have both plans approved, stating that "the Big Bear Lake Park District Board would ask for bids on both the original and alternate plans and would undoubtedly accept the lowest bid."[38]

The first set of plans was for a traveling cable–type lift, whereas the second set of plans was for a trolley-type lift. The Forest Service approved the plans for the traveling cable–type lift, but both designs were fraught with problems. Discussing the trolley lift, C.B. Morse, assistant regional forester, wrote, "We are glad the Big Bear Lake Park District officials have abandoned the idea of using this particular design. The plans submitted are entirely inadequate and considerable engineering work would be required by them, in working up satisfactory details."[39]

After approval of the traveling cable–type lift, bids for construction were opened on October 10, 1940. But there continued to be ongoing discussion between the State Division of Engineering, the Forest Service and the Big Bear Lake Park District Board regarding the design and safety of the chairlift.

At this time, Sugar Bowl operated the only chairlift in California. The design for the Lynn Lift was similar to the Mount Hood chairlift, so the Division of Engineering was basing the feasibility, performance and safety of the chairlift on that design.

The rudimentary era of chairlift design is evidenced by concerns expressed by the Division of Engineering: "We are not familiar with this type of lift and have never seen one in operation. Due to patents on the chair, it is not possible for the contractor to furnish several pertinent points in operation. Thus it is possible that some of our basic load assumptions might be too great, but we have tried to give the benefit of the doubt to the design."[40]

Once design and safety features were deemed satisfactory, approval to begin construction was given on October 24, 1940. But a problem of a different sort delayed construction. In November 1940, the state attorney general ruled against construction because

> *the law states that such a park district can not construct improvements on land outside the boundaries of such a district. There is a clause in the law, however, that states in effect that if such improvements serve the general public as a whole and can not be located within the district, an exception may be made. It is now planned that the Big Bear Park District secure the aid of State Senator Swing in securing special dispensation in this particular case through the State Legislature. Therefore, action on this particular case will be held in abeyance until legislative action succeeds or fails.*[41]

Then, when World War II began, plans came to a standstill. The Forest Service notified the park board that the Special Use Permit "could not be used until postwar conditions made it possible for the district to erect the structure anticipated and approved in your lease papers."[42]

The prewar estimate for the cost of lift construction was between $15,000 and $18,000. In the early days of the war, money was available for the project, but the price of steel skyrocketed during the war. At least $25,000 would be required to fund the project. Then the availability of steel and materials was restricted, and prices continued to spiral higher and higher. By the time the war was over, the cost had ballooned to $48,000.

In June 1948, Lynn renewed his efforts to get chairlift construction started. The Park Board had $45,000 available, but bids were twice that amount. Not to be deterred, Lynn began contacting local firms regarding the project. Dick Cannon, engineer for Coast Builders in Santa Monica, assured Lynn the lift could be built with the funds available.

September 24, 1949, marked the formal dedication of the chairlift. The ceremony also served as somewhat of a memorial to Lynn. In April 1949, the Big Bear Winter Club hosted a contest to name Big Bear's first chairlift. The contest was publicized in the *San Bernardino Sun* and other local newspapers, encouraging a large number of entries. The contest closed on May 15, and the Winter Club hoped to find "a proper name for this area suggesting the beauty and grandeur of the new county chairlift site, and its wonderful slopes and snow conditions."[43] But when Lynn took his own life in August 1949, the lift was named in his memory.[44]

District commissioners, county officials and members of the press were on hand for the historic event. Local residents were invited and given free rides

Gene Merwin (left), designer of the Lynn Lift, with lift engineer Dick Cannon. The Lynn Lift was Big Bear Lake's first chairlift and the fourth in Southern California. Southern California's first three chairlifts were built at Mount Waterman, Blue Ridge and Snow Valley. *Photo by Wolfgang Lert.*

The Lynn Lift opened to much fanfare on September 24, 1949. Bill Kingsley, president of the Big Bear Lake Park Board, takes a ceremonial ride on the historic day. *Photo by Wolfgang Lert.*

on the lift. The magnitude of Lynn's contribution to Big Bear Lake winter sports was conveyed in the dedication speech:

> *Clifford Roy Lynn dedicated his life and services securing realization of his dreams, of his vision to make Big Bear a winter sports field second to none. He worked unceasingly—often in a single handed battle against great odds—because of his conviction that winter sports at Big Bear could be the finest in the west if proper facilities were made available to the public... Today it is just and fitting that we dedicate the Clifford Lynn Chair Lift to the memory of one who visioned for Big Bear leadership as the winter sports center of the west, and took upon himself the obligation of securing the means to that end.*[45]

A view of the Lynn Lift base area on opening day, September 24, 1949. *Photo by Wolfgang Lert.*

At the time of its completion, it was one of fewer than ten chairlifts in the nation and operated in both winter and summer. Tyndall's Big Bear Winter Club enthusiastically began promoting all of Big Bear's ski tows and all manner of winter sports. The club created a postcard, the front showing Tyndall's map of the local winter sports areas and the verso giving a vivid description of the Big Bear winter sports scene:

> *Here are the "bear" facts about the new chairlift at Big Bear. What a deal! Park-Board operated—carrying 240 skiers per hour…up over beautiful snow to almost 8000 ft. elevation. Skiers from all over Southern California are thrilled. Beginners learn in ski school on broad, easy slopes at the top. Experts schuss and swoop on steep, exciting runs all the way down. What's more, there are 8 other good ski areas in Big Bear now (see map)—plus a dozen tows including the familiar sling lift on "Old County." No other area around offers such a variety of winter sports so close to a community of 7000 pop. We sponsor tobogganing, movies, ice skating, bowling, and dancing. All this and accommodations too! So many resorts, lodges, hotels, cafes, and bars it's hard to choose. Plus regular bus transportation—Mt. Auto Lines, Tanner Motors, and Greyhound. This is the place. Come up and "ski" for yourself…only 3 hours drive from Los Angeles—4 from San Diego. Hitch hike if you have to. It's worth it. See you soon…*[46]

The inaugural season was a great success but was not without some problems. On October 30, 1949, the cable dropped off the sheaves at tower nine, dropping six passengers to the snowless ground. Miraculously, only one of the riders was injured. The chair she was riding was demolished.

Because of this accident, the Lynn Lift was inspected in July 1950 by the Engineering Department of the Pacific Indemnity Company. Its report was severe. It stated:

> *Close investigation now indicates the fact that the pulley wheels are splitting the axles. From all indications, there is a great deal of vibration set up in the pulley constellations when the chair lift clamps pass through these pulleys. This vibration, coupled with the heavy cable stress, is bound to continually break out at some point, with the constant possibility of riders becoming injured through failure at one of these points.*
>
> *It is my considered opinion that a major overhaul of the entire set-up along the following lines will be necessary before it can be considered a safe, standard chair lift:*

> 1. *A re-survey of the profile should be made and some of the towers placed in a different location in order to flatten out the cable travel and eliminate some of the stresses which it now develops.*
> 2. *Towers should be anchored more firmly and X-braced with angle iron, rather that flat strap iron.*
> 3. *They should use one of the standard pulley arrangements which would eliminate some of the vibration caused by the present cable clamps.*
> 4. *The towers should be screened or shielded on the one side to eliminate the possibility of the skis getting hooked into them.*
> 5. *A guide should be installed around the No. 1 tower and motor house to prevent the chairs from smashing into the building.*[47]

In September 1950, the San Bernardino County Board of Supervisors approved the use of $5,000 for the required repairs. D.W. Kingsley, chairman of the Big Bear Lake Park Board, explained that with the appointment of Bill Franklin and Don Dawson to the park board commission,

> *the county feels that the district is now in an excellent position to manage the lift. The board now has engineering ability, mechanical ability, and funds. Mr. Franklin engineered the original plans for a chair lift at Big Bear. However, they were never used because the engineering called for a project more costly than the district felt it could undertake, but they have subsequently been endorsed as the only feasible chair lift plans by such authorities as noted chair lift construction firms.*[48]

The other major problem was access to and parking at the area. The completion of the Lynn Lift resulted in an influx of winter sports visitors, and road conditions to the area were narrow, steep and dangerous. To alleviate the parking problem, the Big Bear Lake Park Board issued a request to the San Bernardino County Board of Supervisors to purchase the "area comprising Lots 43-44-46-47 and 48, Pine Knot Subdivision No. 2…by condemnation if necessary, also, of the donated easement consisting of a fifty (50) foot wide right of way, a continuation of Pine Knot Boulevard extending from Oak Street south to Cameron Drive, approximately 1500 feet in length."[49] This plan would have accommodated four hundred cars within a five-hundred-foot radius of the chairlift and would have served skiers using both the chairlift and the sling lift.

Local residents objected to this proposal, so the plan never gained approval from the Board of Supervisors. In March 1951, the Park Board requested permission to purchase two acres of land from W.A. Dermid for the purpose of developing a parking area at the Lynn Lift.

A winter view of the Lynn Lift. The historic single chair operated for more than thirty years until it was finally removed in 1981.

The popularity of the lift continued to grow over the years and led to long lift lines on busy weekends, with skiers sometimes enduring a forty-minute wait. In its first three seasons of operation, the lift carried six thousand summer and winter passengers. The lift also benefited local businesses, with some businesses reporting that income tripled after the lift went into operation.

The completion of the chairlift was just the beginning of the development of the area, and improvements continued throughout the 1949–50 season. The Big Bear Winter Club held slope-clearing parties, and after the snow fell, the Park Board realized that it needed an additional tow for beginners. In January 1950, it installed a rope tow for access to the "bunny bowl" at the top of the chairlift. With the seven-hundred-foot rope tow, beginners could ride the chairlift to the bowl, ski the bunny bowl with uphill access via the rope tow and then at the end of the day ride the chairlift back down without having to ski over steep runs lower on the hill. Prior to the installation of the rope tow, beginners were limited to using the sling lift or other beginner tows in the valley, but they now had access to the deep powder that sometimes blanketed the higher slopes.

The Lynn Lift underwent additional upgrades during the 1950–51 season. *The Skier* described the improvements: "Number two run is now smooth and wide all the way down—a beauty for intermediates starting at nearly 8000 feet and gliding down for over a mile to the chairlift terminal at 7000 feet.

'Steilhang' on Number one expert run has also been widened, and at the top of the chair, the contour of the Bunny tow has been changed so the rope rides high and dry."[50]

In addition to the upgrades made to the Lynn Lift area, the sling lift slopes also underwent big changes. A road now connected the two areas, which permitted skiers to be transported by weasels from the village. For skiers driving to the area, the access road was improved and parking capacity increased.

Also at this time, Tommi Tyndall and Hank Smith's Big Bear Certified Ski School became more organized and prominent. A large area at the bottom terminal of the Lynn Lift was cleared and marked specifically for ski school use. They added a Jeep-driven tow that carried beginners up a long, gentle slope. This tow was installed for the exclusive use of the ski school. And for the first time, the Park Board and the Big Bear Certified Ski School signed a contract, signifying complete cooperation between the two organizations.

As Snow Summit and other Big Bear Lake ski areas were developed in the early to mid-1950s, the Park Board began to have reservations about conducting a business that competed directly with private ski area owners. In a letter dated October 30, 1956, A.P. Tidwell, chairman of the Big Bear Lake Park Board, wrote to the Board of Supervisors asking them to consider the sale of the winter sports facilities operated by the Park District. He explained that private ski area operators "have entered the winter sports field on a large scale in Big Bear Valley, meeting the needs of winter recreation enthusiasts of Southern California," and that "it is not in the best interest of the community to continue to operate winter sports facilities in competition with private enterprises." He went on to explain that the Lynn Lift area had "fulfilled its original function of fostering growth of winter sports facilities in Big Bear Valley."

This was not the first time local ski tow operators voiced concern over unfair competition with the county-owned Lynn Lift. In a 1950 letter to the County Park Board, a group of ski area operators wrote:

> *We, the undersigned, owners of private ski tows, vigorously protest the use of taxpayer's funds for this purpose* [construction of a new rope tow]. *We believe that any further investment of County funds in competition to us is a decided infringement upon our rights and the rights and privileges of private enterprise and management. We, endeavoring to earn a living in a field already practically monopolized by the County Park Board, are directly competing with a business subsidized by the monies paid by us and other taxpayers of Bear Valley.*
>
> *While we independent ski tow operators must depend on our actual earnings to exist and to make improvements upon our investments, the County*

> *facilities may pour more funds into improvements each year, without having earned these funds. If this continues, it is inevitable that private industry will be forced out of the ski tow business in Bear Valley.*[51]

The letter was signed by John Sipe, Upper and Lower Mill Creek Ski Bowls; Virgil Foust, Swiss Ski Tows; Max Files, Lone Star Ski Tow; and Bill Goold, Snow White Ski Tow.

The county put the area on the auction block on May 28, 1957. The Park Board recommended a minimum bid of $125,000.[52] No bids were received and Forest Service officials suspected two reasons: the lack of snow the previous year and spring being the wrong time of the year to try to sell a winter sports area.

A second attempt to sell the area was initiated on October 2, 1962. The County Board of Supervisors voted unanimously to authorize the Big Bear Lake Park Board to call for bids for the sale of the area. The minimum bid was set at $75,000.

The county continued to own and operate the lift through the end of 1962. Then, in January 1963, Edward Blacker and J. Edwin Spangler, the sole bidders, acquired the area for $75,000. Spangler had owned and operated his own businesses and had experience managing more than 150 employees. Blacker was a partner in the Black & Blacker real estate firm in Pasadena, where he had been a successful broker for more than thirty-two years.

Immediately after the purchase, Blacker and Spangler applied for incorporation under the name of EBES Enterprises, Inc. However, in March, completion of the sale was delayed for thirty days because the pair was waiting for the approval of the Securities and Exchange Commission to sell stock. Then, in early April, the pair backed out of the deal, claiming that financing fell through because of "death, sickness and poor snow conditions."[53]

Brothers Dave and Dan Platus became the new owners in April 1963 and renamed it Snow Forest. Snow Forest was made up of two separate and distinct areas. The lower portion, the Lynn Lift area, was outfitted with the single chairlift, one rope tow, a cafeteria, ski rentals, a ski shop and a ski school. Facilities at the upper area, known as Little Siberia, included four rope tows, a snack bar, ski rentals, a ski shop and a ski school.

The brothers immediately began making improvements. Snow making was first on the list, and by December 1963, a snow-making system was in place on Little Siberia and the twenty-five-year-old sling lift was replaced with a rope tow. Because of their new snow-making system, the 1963–64 season was expanded to ninety-four days, more than doubling a typical season without snow making.

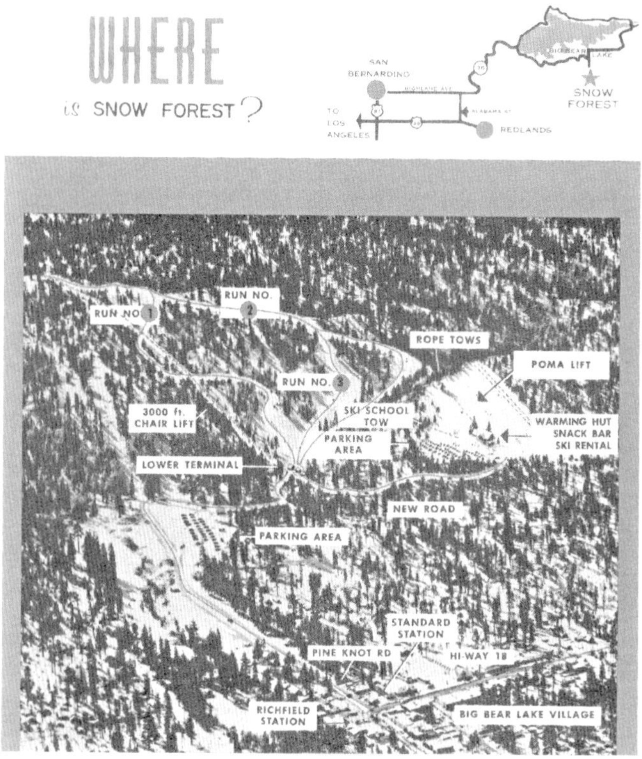

A map of Snow Forest showing how two distinct areas were fashioned into one. The area to the right had been known as Little Siberia, while the other area was simply known as the Lynn Lift.

In spite of increased skier days, Snow Forest was in the red by the end of the Platuses' second season at the helm. Forest Service officer D.M. Tucker spelled out the difficulties Snow Forest faced:

> *The cold truth, as I see it, is that at present this area is hard to find, hard to see, and the slopes much less attractive than Snow Summit. Due to County operation, with no competitive incentive, the permittee is faced with a job of attracting customers away from Snow Valley, Snow Summit, and Moonridge. This will require 3–5 years to attract customers through a bold advertising campaign. Next, improvements and slopes must be competitive with other winter sports areas. Increasing interest in skiing may help this situation. Investors will have to wait for 3–5 years before a return can be expected.*[54]

Snow Forest acquired additional acreage next to Little Siberia and was in a position to undertake significant improvements to the area prior to the 1967–68 season. But in March 1967, the Forest Service began to push for the removal of the Lynn Lift because of considerable erosion problems on the slopes served by the chairlift. This became a point of contention between the Forest Service and Snow Forest. Dan Platus wrote:

> *It has been concluded by Snow Forest, Inc. that expansion of its Siberia area with the installation of a major lift facility accessible from the main highway entering Big Bear Lake Village represents the most expedient means of developing Snow Forest into a competitive winter sports area. Further development of its existing Lynn Chairlift area will require reevaluation pending some operating experience with the expanded Siberia area.*[55]

The Forest Service, however, did not want the development of any new facilities on Little Siberia and the adjacent 160 acres until the Lynn Lift was removed. The Platuses felt that the Lynn Lift was too important to their business to remove it in the three to five years recommended by the Forest Service. They wanted to develop Little Siberia before the removal of the Lynn Lift. In a letter to the district ranger, Dan Platus spelled out Snow Forest's position:

> *The immediate objective of Snow Forest, Inc. is to conduct a profitable or at least self-sustaining winter sports operation while providing an important service needed by the National Forest using public. It is believed that this may be possible with the existing facilities either in their present condition, or with perhaps some limited improvement to the Little Siberia Area such as the addition of a Poma or platter lift on the existing ski slope. While it is our ultimate objective to consolidate the operation on the Little Siberia Area, we must rely on existing facilities until such time that they are not needed. It is most certain that the present operation could not be sustained without the existing Lynn Chairlift…Based on the operation on natural snow during the past two seasons, the chairlift accounted for 45.5% and 49.9%, respectively, of the total revenue from lift and tow tickets. In the event that the chairlift were not operated, the total yearly operating cost would be reduced very little, yet this major source of revenue would be eliminated.*[56]

After several written exchanges and meetings, a new Special Use Permit was agreed upon on October 23, 1967, and Snow Forest was able to complete the installation of a new one-thousand-foot Poma lift at Little Siberia in time for the 1967–68 season.

But money woes continued to plague the business. In September 1968, the San Bernardino County Board of Supervisors decided to foreclose on Snow Forest. The brothers had not kept up with payments or paid taxes on the area.

However, two months later, the board voted to allow the brothers to operate for the coming winter while financial difficulties were being worked out.

Snow Forest survived the foreclosure threat, and in January 1970, a Development Plan and Program was submitted to the Forest Service. The installation of Chairlift No. 2 during the 1970–71 season was of the utmost importance to Snow Forest management. That chairlift would have served the entire Little Siberia bowl, and Dan Platus explained, "We are undertaking this project at a time when the economic climate places great financial burden on each Snow Forest shareholder. The risks are required however because this development is so essential to the basic objective of attaining a financially profitable operation while at the same time providing a good public service."[57]

In April 1972, the Board of Directors of Snow Forest, Inc. decided to put the area up for sale. They concluded that they did not have the capital necessary to develop the area into a self-sustaining or profitable business. The Platuses continued to operate the area, and during the 1972–73 season, the old Lynn Lift suffered several accidents, structural failures and malfunctions. It is remarkable that the Lynn Lift was still in operation. As early as June 1957, Jack Kilsky of the Division of Industrial Safety noted that the "chair lift was in bad condition and would need to be replaced next year."[58]

The problems with the lift forced Snow Forest to request non-use for the 1973–74 season. They were not able to make the necessary upgrades to the lift and felt that too much revenue would be lost without its operation. Snow Forest remained closed through the 1976–77 season. The owners had invested a substantial amount of money in the area over the years, and efforts to secure a buyer for the area continued even while the tows and chairlift sat idle.

In September 1977, Ken Lieb, a longtime skier and certified public accountant, purchased Snow Forest. Then, in November 1977, he purchased nearby Magic Mountain, with plans to combine the two areas into one 190-acre area called Crystal Ridge Ski Area. He served as president of the Crystal Ridge Corporation, established in July 1977. In addition to Lieb, stockholders included Arnold Snitser, Carole Evans, Pete Pecarovich, Wilbur Petrick, Howard Jenkins III, Frank Genova and Robert Brown.

Lieb had extensive plans for his new area. The old lifts were to be removed and replaced with five chairlifts, one Poma lift and two rope tows. An extensive snow-making system was included in the plan, as well as increased parking and base lodge facilities. One of the proposed lifts extended beyond the permit boundary, which would add an additional twenty acres to the Snow Forest area.

In July 1978, as negotiations for Snow Forest continued, Lieb made plans to install two portable Poma lifts and two rope tows on the property at Magic Mountain and did not plan to open Crystal Ridge until the 1978–79 ski season. He was awaiting the completion of the Special Use Permit for Crystal Ridge and permission to install a snow-making pond. The Forest Service doubted that Lieb could meet the financial requirements of his Special Use Permit since the Small Business Administration declined his loan request and a source of additional financing fell through.

The negotiations for the sale of Snow Forest to Crystal Ridge were terminated in August 1978, but Lieb was still interested in obtaining the permit for Snow Forest, pending proof of his financial ability to operate and develop the area with mutually acceptable terms with Snow Forest, Inc.

However, the Forest Service still had doubts about Lieb's plans and his ability to bankroll those plans. The acting forest supervisor wrote, "There continues to be a question as to whether Crystal Ridge can qualify financially for a Special Use Permit. If not, Snow Forest is anxious to place their facilities back on the market, if a permit is not forthcoming to Crystal Ridge."[59] After review, the Forest Service concluded that it saw "no positive indications that the corporation would be able to handle the proposed development cost of approximately $750,000."[60]

During the fall of 1979, the U.S. Forest Service issued an edict for the Platus brothers to either revive Snow Forest or forfeit their permit, so they reopened for the 1979–80 season. Three factors influenced their decision to open the area: "A very favorable arrangement with the forest service as well as increased financial backing; needed room to expand and a tremendous increase in the number of ski enthusiasts."[61]

The area opened without the use of the Lynn Lift because of the chairlift's age and poor condition. The initial cost of start-up was small because existing facilities could be remodeled rather than having to build new structures from scratch.

The Platus brothers continued as owners and operators and, in 1980, acquired a new business partner, Bob Boothe. Catering to the novice skier, the owners advertised Little Siberia as a "10-acre ski hill serviced by a 1000-foot long Poma lift, three rope tows, 100 percent snowmaking, and 100 percent snow grooming. All runs are geared for learning skiers; no schussboomers or competing with advanced or expert skiers."[62]

Boothe acted as general manager until he bought the area from the brothers later that season. He also purchased the adjacent Crystal Ridge area. Finally, in 1981, the thirty-two-year-old Lynn Lift was removed and was later replaced with a new three-thousand-foot-long triple chairlift with a six-hundred-foot vertical rise. The triple chair, which debuted on January 6, 1982, had an uphill capacity of 1,800 skiers per hour.

When Snow Forest opened for the 1981–82 season, it was actually three areas in one. The new triple chair provided access for the Lynn Lift hill; a

Dave and Dan Platus bought the Lynn Lift area in April 1963 and named it Snow Forest. Once the Lynn Lift was removed, construction began on a triple chair. A helicopter was indispensable in transporting and placing lift towers. The triple chair opened on January 6, 1982. The old Lynn Lift had an uphill capacity of 240 skiers per hour. The new triple chair carried 1,800 skiers per hour. *Courtesy of Ray Ransom.*

Poma lift and three rope tows served Little Siberia; and a platter tow and two rope tows operated on the slopes of Crystal Ridge. The entire area now had a two-thousand-skier capacity.

Snow Forest underwent significant improvements for the 1983–84 season. Prior to this time, the chairlift only serviced runs designed for advanced skiers. The Lynn Mountain run was only twenty feet wide but was widened to three hundred feet. Fifteen acres of new terrain were added to the area, and major upgrading took place on some of the existing runs. Because of the extensive improvements, Snow Forest was named the Far West Ski Association's "Outstanding Ski Area of the Year" for 1984. It was also given the Tommi Tyndall award for making a distinguished contribution to skiing.

Snow Forest was an ideal area for beginners. Advanced skiers seeking more challenging terrain passed it by. The longest run was only three-quarters of a mile, the vertical drop just eight hundred feet. At one time, owners hoped that Snow Forest could be developed so that they could compete with nearby Snow Summit and Goldmine. But in its more than forty-year history, the Lynn Lift–Snow Forest area seldom operated in the black. Don R. Bauer, forest supervisor, summarized the difficulties that Snow Forest faced:

> *Through the years with the development of other winter sites on nearby National Forest and private lands, the old Lynn lift and its successor Snow Forest, Inc. have been unable to remain competitive in this highly competitive field, and at the same time fulfill the terms of the special use permit agreement. A clear cut public need for the expanded facilities as proposed by Snow Forest Inc. no longer exists in this area. Superior opportunities for expansion of "high lift ski operations" exist nearby. Both Snow Summit and Moonridge areas are capable of and have plans for expansion in addition to new areas which can be developed should the public need and availability of private investment capital warrant.*[63]

Snow Forest closed permanently in 1992.

Even after the area closed, the Forest Service continued to receive inquiries about reviving the area. Its fate was officially sealed in 1993. According to Paul Bennett, U.S. Forest Service district winter sports administrator, "The district has had various inquiries regarding the possible reissuance of a Special Use Permit for the area. However, at this time I believe there is no need to provide additional skiing and snowboarding opportunities for the public in the Big Bear area."[64]

Bennett felt that the area, if revived, would not be economically viable. The area had a long history of financial troubles and over the years had been on the edge of financial collapse. Bob Boothe, who was the last permittee for the area, had filed for personal and corporate bankruptcy.

During the 1990s, all of the buildings, along with the chairlift and rope tows, were removed from the site. The former slopes that once were home to the unique sling lift and Big Bear Lake's first chairlift now sit empty and barren. And even though the ski tows last carried skiers up the historic hill twenty years ago, in 2006, the Forest Service was still confronting substantial erosion issues at the area.

Rebel Ridge

Chuck Smith founded Rebel Ridge in the fall of 1955, and in a January 1956 ski column in the *Los Angeles Times*, Glen Binford referred to Rebel Ridge as "a really hustling, comparatively new spot just beyond Big Bear."[65] Smith had worked for Tommi Tyndall at Snow Summit, but the two did not always see eye to eye. Their disagreements led Smith to name his area "Rebel Ridge." He chose an area located on a small north-facing ridge on the west boundary of Big Bear City. By its second year of operation, Rebel Ridge was the only Big Bear area offering night skiing, available on Friday and Saturday nights.

Smith operated four rope tows serving five acres of clear, open slopes: one 1,500-foot, two 900-foot and one 600-foot beginner tow. The area was also outfitted with two toboggan runs and a warming hut.

The resort was unique in that the slopes were carefully bulldozed for each class of skier, up to advanced intermediates. They were arranged so each class of skier skied within his or her own boundaries, eliminating the schussboomer traffic from the top of the hill into the beginners' area. Ed Heath, brother of 1936 Olympian Clarita Heath Bright, helped Smith lay out the terrain. Heath, hired on as the ski school director, felt Rebel Ridge had one of the top teaching areas in Southern California.

Smith experimented with snow making at Rebel Ridge as early as 1956.[66] In his first attempt, he hoped to cover an area one hundred by eight hundred feet with eight inches of snow. He installed two-inch water mains and used a hose borrowed from the local fire department.

Through the New Year weekend of the 1960–61 season, Rebel Ridge was the only ski area open west of the Mississippi.[67] Daytime temperatures were balmy, but nighttime temperatures sometimes dropped lower than twenty-eight degrees, the temperature that Smith calculated to be the magic number for snow making. On those occasions, he kept his pumps, pipes and nozzles running all night. The dry, pine-covered hills became blanketed with snow. Four to six inches of fresh, natural powder blanketed the man-made base that had been sprayed on the slopes previously. His system was large enough to keep two runs open.

Skiers knew where to find the only snow in Southern California, and their cars filled the parking lot. The two nine-hundred-foot rope tows carried the snow-starved skiers to the top of the hill. Neither of the runs was especially long (a little less than a quarter mile) or steep, but these New Year's skiers were thrilled just to find some snow. *Skiing* magazine gave an apt description of the Rebel Ridge scene during those early snow-making years: "In the dusty parking lot, two girls in Bermuda shorts and short-sleeved shirts posed for pictures in a 70-degree sun. The background: A snow-covered slope 100 yards away."[68]

Prior to the advent of snow making, Rebel Ridge had averaged fewer than thirty days per season, but now it could provide skiing from November to March. However, Smith's system was labor intensive. Each sprinkler sprayed snow over approximately one hundred square feet, so he and his crew were busy all night moving hoses and sprinklers. But Smith said, "It's worth it when you take the first run of the morning through that powder."[69]

Though others in the West had experimented with snow making prior to this time (Les Salm in the Lake Arrowhead area in the 1940s and Smith at

Snow-covered slopes surrounded by pine needles was a familiar scene at Rebel Ridge in the early 1960s. A pioneer in Southern California snow making, Chuck Smith blanketed the slopes with "custom snow" when nighttime temperatures and conditions permitted. When there was a lack of natural snow, Rebel Ridge was sometimes the only Southland ski area operating thanks to Smith's man-made snow.

Moonridge in the mid-1950s), Rebel Ridge was the first area in the West to successfully implement snow making, and the "custom snow," as Smith called it, grabbed the attention of local skiers and ski area operators.[70]

Smith continued to upgrade his snow-making system, and other ski areas took a keen interest. "Rebel Ridge was an eye opener to the benefits of snow making, not only in Southern California but areas in other states as well."[71] Machine snow making guaranteed an early start to the ski season. Areas that had snow making could open in mid-November, while areas without this capability remained idle. Other ski area operators must have known that this could be the answer to Southern California's fickle weather and sometimes nonexistent snowfall. Tommi Tyndall certainly took notice and installed snow making at Snow Summit by 1964.[72]

Rebel Ridge's success with snow making marked a turning point in Southern California ski history. *Ski World* reported:

> *1964 may go into the books as the year that technology supplanted wishful thinking as far as local lift and tow operators are concerned. They have decided, almost unanimously, that artificial snow—costly and limited as it is—is the answer to the chronic lack of natural snow. Five of the local*

ski resorts are introducing snow-making systems this year; two more plan to continue with their existing systems; two are definitely interested but don't plan anything yet; three are stymied by water shortage.[73]

Rebel Ridge also underwent a complete face-lift for the 1960–61 season. Slopes were widened and reshaped, tows were relocated and upgraded and a separate area with a toboggan lift was created for non-skiers.

Then, in July 1963, Stu and Liese Hirsh bought Rebel Ridge. They increased snow making by 30 percent and installed a new platter lift on the west side of the area. They added a new rental shop, repair shop, ski shop and the Rebeler Bar and remodeled the restaurant.

In November 1964, the Hirshes invested $50,000 in a brand-new chairlift. This was Big Bear Lake's third chairlift and second double chair. The 750-foot-long chairlift was equipped with thirty chairs and carried nine hundred skiers per hour. Swiss Freddie Schmutz, well-known ski lift designer and builder, supervised lift construction. The construction of the lift was a joint venture among Schmutz, Allied Cable Ways and American Cable Ways. Skiers now

Sepp Benedikter (far right) created an alpine touch to promote his newly purchased Rebel Ridge. Benedikter had been a longtime ski instructor, racer, ski event organizer and ski lift builder. He became a ski area owner and operator when he purchased Rebel Ridge in December 1965.

had access to the fourteen-acre area, often covered with "custom snow," via the comfort of the new chairlift.[74]

The Hirshes' ownership was short-lived. Sepp Benedikter bought the business in December 1965 and immediately began his own rejuvenation of the area. He installed a new rope tow running from the upper terminal of the chairlift to the top, doubling the length of the run. Benedikter also bulldozed a new slope for a slalom course.

When the 1966–67 season began, Rebel Ridge sported a new $50,000 snow-making system. The snow-making system increased from twenty-one guns to thirty. Benedikter noted that the new snow-making system "makes it possible to guarantee a minimum of six inches of powdered snow from Thanksgiving to April."[75]

Wanting to attract families to the area, Benedikter created a ski school specifically to cater to families, including lessons for children as young as three. Summing up the focus on families, Benedikter said, "We intend to make Rebel Ridge one of the best family-type skiing resorts in Southern California. And in our advertising and among our contacts, we will emphasize the family specializations we offer."[76]

Benedikter began teaching skiing at the age of sixteen in Austria and started a multi-area ski school in Southern California in 1946, serving Blue Ridge, Table Mountain, Mount Waterman and Snow Valley. He was well known among the Hollywood crowd and was often enlisted as an instructor to the stars. Ann Margaret was one of the many stars who signed on for a lesson with Sepp.

An artist's rendering of the master plan Benedikter hoped to carry out at Rebel Ridge. The proposal included a twenty-room lodge, fifty motel rooms, a one-hundred-bed dorm, a sauna, a pool and a boat dock. His dream was never realized, probably due to lack of capital to invest in the project.

The old site of Rebel Ridge as it looked in the summer of 2011. One of the resort's original buildings still stands in the parking lot, unused and boarded up. The area now operates as Big Bear Snow Play, outfitted with a modern building and a magic carpet providing easy, uphill transportation for customers.

Benedikter had ambitious plans for the future of the area. His project called for "50 motel units and a 20-room lodge across the highway, with a 100-bed dormitory, sauna baths, a pool with glass sides and sliding roof for year-round use and a boat dock at the lake for guests."[77] Work on the master plan was to begin in the spring. It is not known what stymied the project, but none of the work was ever begun.

Benedikter sold the area in 1969, and the area permanently closed in 1974. After being shuttered for more than twenty years, the area was revived as a snow play and tubing area in 2000. Big Bear Snow Play, with a lone Rebel Ridge building still standing in its parking lot, continued to successfully operate as of winter 2011.

Other Big Bear Lake Areas

The popularity of the Big Bear Lake sling lift was the impetus for others to install ski tows, and in the 1940s and 1950s, rope tows sprung up just about anywhere there was a north-facing slope of sufficient pitch and length.

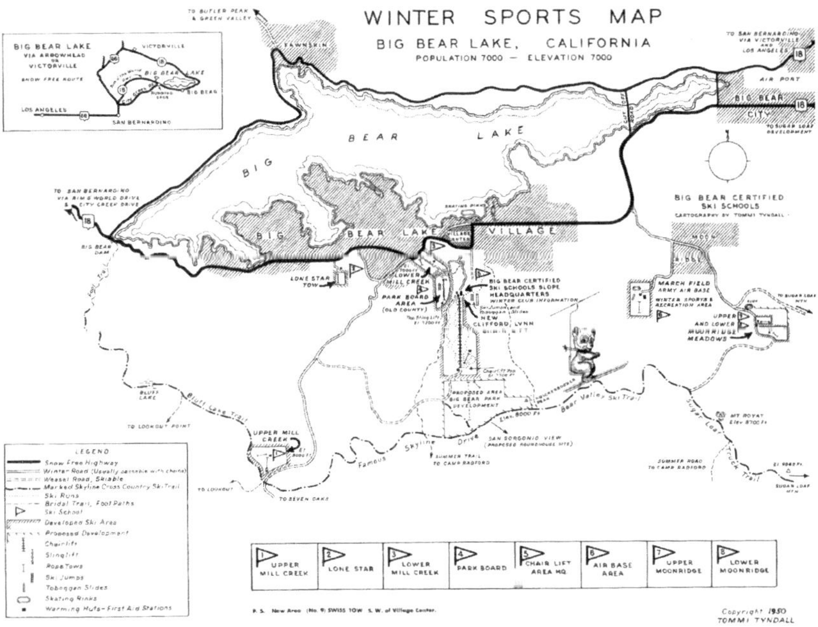

Tommi Tyndall was intimately familiar with Big Bear Lake's many ski areas, having extensively explored Big Bear's surrounding mountains. In 1950, Tyndall created this map of the local winter sports areas.

John Webster and John Sipe installed rope tows at Upper and Lower Mill Creek Ski Bowls, probably in 1947. Upper Mill Creek Ski Bowl, located at 8,000 feet, was outfitted with ski tows of 800, 500 and 150 feet.

Webster and Sipe made additional improvements to the two areas in the fall of 1948. They cleared trees and brush from four large trails. At the same time, the Mill Creek Ski Club came into being, directed by W.H. McEwen, John Webster, John Sipe, Tommi Tyndall, Hank Smith, Barney Rief, Johnny Walp, Mary Ellen Webster and Dick Murphy. The club was not a social club; its primary purpose was to promote skiing and all winter sports in Big Bear Valley.

Upper and Lower Mill Creek Ski Bowls were quite popular. While organizing his Mill Creek Ski School in the fall of 1948, Tyndall had high praise for the area: "Mill Creek is not the name of a place. To all good skiers it is synonymous with good snow conditions. The slopes at Mill Creek are famed for having long lasting snow. The name 'Mill Creek' is a magic word meaning snow as late as April."[78]

Tyndall's Mill Creek Ski School was unique because skiers could sign up for a week of ski instruction that included "24 hours of actual study, four of

A brochure advertising Mill Creek Ski Area, the Mill Creek Ski Club and Tommy Tyndall's Mill Creek Ski School, founded in 1948. His ski school served Upper and Lower Mill Creek Ski Bowls, the sling lift and Lynn Lift, Moonridge and Sugarloaf ski areas.

A summer 2011 view of the old Magic Mountain Ski Area. The area originated in 1947 as Lower Mill Creek Ski Bowl, was renamed Little Siberia in the 1950s and in its last incarnation became Magic Mountain Ski Area. Today, the area operates year-round as Alpine Slide at Magic Mountain.

which is indoor instruction and the rest on skis. Arrangements for this study will be made to include lodging, meals, and use of ski tows."[79]

Lower Mill Creek Ski Bowl eventually became Magic Mountain Ski Area. Today, the area, with its double chairlift in operation, is open year-round as Alpine Slide at Magic Mountain.

Ralph Stewart and Virgil Foust built the Swiss Ski Tows near the present Elk's Lodge. The area was outfitted with two ski tows and a warming hut. Bill Goold operated a tow at what he called Snow White near Coldbrook Camp, with longtime Big Bear Lake instructor Norm Bachelor providing ski instruction. A tow operated at March Air Force Base Recreational Facility, presently the U.S. Marine Corps recreation area. And Max Files's Lone Star Tow, two miles west of the village where the present-day city hall sits, was equipped with floodlights for night skiing on Friday and Saturday nights. Two tows operated daily, servicing gentle slopes for beginner and intermediate skiers.

In January 1954, a beginner area with two rope tows opened at Stillwell's, just east of the present-day post office. Stillwell's, built in 1921 by Carl and Charles Stillwell, was considered the most beautiful lodge in Big Bear Lake. The luxurious pavilion was built of native timber and was situated with an impressive view of the lake. Stillwell's rope tows, 250 feet and 100 feet

A brochure for Happy Hill Resort, where winter visitors could find a beginners' rope tow and toboggan and sledding areas.

long, operated on a gentle slope perfect for beginners. Winter sports visitors also had the use of a warming hut, a toboggan run and ski instruction by John Sipe.

Hake's Happy Hill Ski Tow, located in Big Bear near what was then the Lake Drive-in Theatre, operated one tow for beginners and included toboggan and sledding areas.

In the summer of 1948, a $200,000 corporation called Grout Creek Sports, Inc. was formed to create an all-year playground on Grout Creek near Fawnskin.[80] Members of the corporation included Jess Wilson, owner of Wilson's Market in Fawnskin; J.P. McVeigh; Austin Glaze; Ray Kious; and D.W. Gage. The initial master plan for the resort, composed of twenty-six acres near the bridge at Grout Creek, included construction of a recreation center, playground, skating rink, outdoor swimming pool, ski runs, toboggan slides, lodge buildings and clubhouse. The strategy was to bring busloads of college students to the area in both winter and summer at a minimal cost to the students or their colleges—in other words, to do a large volume of business at a small per-person cost.

The original Grout Creek plan was never completed, but by January 1951, a scaled-down Grout Creek Ski and Recreation Area was in business. Manager Jess Wilson oversaw a ski run with a six-hundred-foot rope tow, warming hut, rental equipment, a Scandinavian instructor and food services that offered

A view of Fawnskin's six-hundred-foot-long Grout Creek ski tow, March 4, 1951. *Courtesy of the National Archives at Riverside, Perris, CA.*

sandwiches and coffee. Skiers paid one dollar per day, with parking less than three hundred yards away in Fawnskin. The tow was situated five hundred feet from the stone bridge that crossed Grout Creek west of the village and provided access to a variety of ski runs. However, the Grout Creek area experienced limited success, and the operation was short-lived. Unfortunately, Fawnskin, just at the northern fringe of storms, did not receive sufficient snow to sustain a successful winter sports operation, and most skiers were probably frequenting the already established resorts (the Lynn Lift and Moonridge) on the south side of the lake where snowfall was more reliable.

The small ski areas throughout Big Bear Valley eventually lost skiers to Snow Summit (founded in 1952) and Moonridge (founded in 1943 and now known as Bear Mountain) as those areas became larger and were outfitted with snow making. Skiers were attracted to the higher, longer and more plentiful runs, taking business from small areas without the capital or acreage to expand. By the mid-1950s, unable to compete, many of the small areas that dotted the slopes around Big Bear were eventually forced to close.

Chapter 4
SAN GABRIEL MOUNTAINS

Table Mountain/Ski Sunrise

The area known at its inception as Table Mountain Ski Area, later as Ski Sunrise and today as North Pole Tubing Park is three miles west of Wrightwood and approximately seventy-five miles from Los Angeles. The road leading to the area is directly across the street from Mountain High West (formerly Blue Ridge Ski Area). It was one of the few "upside-down" resorts where skiers parked at the top of the mountain and skied down to catch a lift back up. Beginner slopes were at the top near the parking lot. The intermediate and advanced slopes were at the bottom of the area and could not be seen from the parking lot or day lodge.

Winter sports devotees cross-country skied at Table Mountain as early as the 1920s, and after the Smithsonian Institution built a solar research observatory in 1926 along with a dirt access road, the area attracted an increasing number of skiers.

Harlow "Buzz" Dormer obtained the first Forest Service Special Use Permit to construct a ski tow and warming hut on Table Mountain on January 6, 1939. (He applied for the permit on November 15, 1938.) The Big Pines Ski Club was listed as the permittee, in care of Secretary/Treasurer Harlow Dormer. The venture was specified as non-commercial, and the Forest Service stipulated that charges for the use of the tow could not exceed the minimum operating costs.

Dormer began living in Big Pines in 1934 and worked as assistant chief ranger at Big Pines Park for a number of years. He was an avid outdoorsman and one of a group of fourteen skiers who formed the Big Pines Ski Club on January 2, 1932.[81] (The club was organized on January 2, but its first meeting

The base area of the Table Mountain rope tow, built in early 1939, the first ski tow in the Big Pines area. Harlow Dormer and Craig Wilson operated the tow for almost five years until Howard More took charge of the area in 1945. *Courtesy of Ann Dormer Johnson.*

Rope tow motor and gears that powered the Table Mountain rope tow. *Courtesy of Ann Dormer Johnson.*

Harlow "Buzz" Dormer was an avid outdoorsman and served as the assistant chief ranger for Los Angeles County at Big Pines Park for many years. He and thirteen other skiers formed the Big Pines Ski Club on January 2, 1932. He obtained the first Forest Service Special Use Permit to construct a ski tow and warming hut on Table Mountain on January 6, 1939. *Courtesy of Ann Dormer Johnson.*

was not held until January 9.) The fourteen founding members met at Camp Cienega to work out the details of the club and elect officers. The inaugural officers were Will C. Vaughan, president; Virgil Dahl, vice-president; and Harlow Dormer, secretary and treasurer.

At the club's second meeting, held on January 16, members planned their weekly ski outing, and President Vaughan appointed Bill Harris as captain of the ski jumping classes and Lester LaVelle as captain of the cross-country and mountaineering activities.

Shortly after arriving in Big Pines, Dormer became the official photographer for *Trails Magazine*, beginning with the summer 1934 issue. The magazine was published by the Mountain League of Southern California to promote outdoor recreation, especially in Los Angeles County. It was published quarterly, with the autumn issue usually featuring winter sports. Starting with the autumn 1935 issue, a portion of the magazine was designated as the Big Pines Ski Club Year Book. This typically ran only two pages.

The Big Pines Ski Club had hoped to construct a tow at Table Mountain as early as 1936. It published a notice in the autumn 1936 issue of *Trails Magazine* that it was eager to install a tow on its club grounds. The announcement read, "Feeling the pulse of many of our ski enthusiasts who have but one day a week to ski, and who desire to get in as many rides DOWN the hill as possible in their allotted time, we are attempting to install a power pull-back on the slalom course this winter. We are not promising, but we are pulling."

The popularity and development of winter sports in the Big Pines area and the immediate success and growth of the Big Pines Ski Club (by 1935, the club had 166 members) were due to the efforts and inspiration of Dormer. Members of the Big Pines Ski Club recognized this, and on December 6, 1940, the club granted Dormer an honorary life membership. He had served as club secretary treasurer from the club's inception through December 1940, and the club noted that "he has been probably the greatest inspiration in the development of the Club and has generously donated untold time, energy, and personal money toward that development."[82]

Dormer and Craig Wilson operated the Table Mountain tow for almost five years until, on December 22, 1944, Dormer filed a request to relinquish his Special Use Permit, handing over the ski tow and warming hut to Howard More.[83] More received his Special Use Permit on January 30, 1945, and he didn't waste any time planning improvements for the area. He wrote the Forest Service on February 8, 1945, explaining his ideas:

A simple advertisement for the Table Mountain Ski Tow.

> *Within the approval of the Forest Service and other conditions permitting, the writer would like to expand Table Mountain facilities so that there would be at least three tows, and have the area taken in by this Permit enlarged so as to take in the entire Table Mountain Ski area. The writer would also like to be considered primary applicant for the operation of any recreational facilities installed in this area, such as, lunch and shelter installations, etc.*[84]

More, born on August 2, 1914, in Indianapolis, Indiana, spent his youth in Denver, Colorado. He was introduced to skiing through his involvement with the Boy Scouts. Thor Groswold, of the Groswold Ski Company, led Boy Scout ski trips, and it was on one of these trips with Groswold, in 1926, that More strapped on skis for the first time. More made many other ski trips as a Boy Scout and, while attending South High School in Denver, skied with the Rebel Rangers, a group founded by South High chemistry teacher and mountain guide Bob Collier. The club was popular, with seventy-five to one hundred boys and girls involved in climbing, skiing, hiking and other outdoor activities.

More went on to study at the University of Colorado–Boulder, where he earned a degree in mechanical engineering. He later attended Harvard

Howard More took over operation of the Table Mountain Ski Tow in 1945, marking the beginning of his more than fifty years at the helm. He developed the area into the quintessential family ski area. Renamed Ski Sunrise in 1975, it was purchased by Mountain High Ski Resort in 2004. Mountain High now operates the area as the North Pole Tubing Park.

Business School and, in 1939, received a degree in transportation, with a specialization in railroads. More then landed a job with Alcoa, from which he retired after twenty-five years.

More eventually moved to Southern California, and one winter weekend in 1941, he drove to Mount Waterman, where at least eight feet of snow had accumulated on Cloudburst Summit. It was on this trip that he discovered Table Mountain.

More's first season at the helm of Table Mountain Ski Area was in 1945–46. He had experience at other ski areas and had built rope tows at Seven Springs, Snow Valley and Green Valley Lake, but he credited many other men who were instrumental in helping to build and install equipment: Mac Templeton, Frank Jones, Forest Supervisor Bill Mendenhall, District Ranger Charles Beardsley, Cliff Plank and many U.S. Forest Service personnel. Buddy Rowe, Milt Sayle and Elmer Sayle milled the Jeffrey pines into lumber for the day lodge, and Mike Yarborough and Gil Gillard built the massive chimney. Area managers Bob and Erma Waag played a critical role in keeping the operation running smoothly. In the 1950s, Jean Pomagalski traveled from France to install Poma lifts.

The Table Mountain day lodge shortly after it was constructed. Built during the 1952–53 season, it featured a large outdoor deck with desert and mountain views, a large fireplace, a rental shop and a food and beverage area.

The popularity of Table Mountain Ski Area, especially after World War II, was evident in a note that More sent to the Forest Service in June 1949: "As near as I can calculate, we entertained 6,600 visitors 90% of whom were hauled, mainly by weasel, from the Arch. The road was closed practically the whole season. We operated a total of 40 days (17 weekends) which is some sort of a record for Table Mt."[85]

By 1960, Table Mountain skiers could roam the area via two Poma lifts and seven rope tows. One Poma, 2,200 feet long with a vertical rise of 754 feet, was claimed to be California's largest at the time. The lift served an area with fantastic views of the Mojave Desert. This slope was smoothed into a vast bowl, adding challenging terrain for expert skiers. Intermediate skiers had access to a long ridge and wide, clear trails that led down to the lower terminal of the lift. The other Poma lift, 2,000 feet long with a 350-foot rise, gave access to intermediate and beginner runs.

In 1973, More sold Table Mountain to Tamount, Inc., a group of four investors. Tamount appointed Dave Ward as new general manager of the area, and in 1975, he changed the name of the area to Ski Sunrise. The name was meant to convey a new dawning for the area, which for many years had been overshadowed by Mountain High across the highway.

Ward planned to install a new triple chair, Ski Sunrise's first chairlift, prior to the 1977–78 season. Workers prepared foundation holes and readied the area for construction, but the lift manufacturer reneged on its promise to deliver all of the lift components by the end of October 1977. Ward finally got his new chair in 1979. Instead of the planned triple chair, he installed a Riblet quad chair. The new lift, 1,550 feet long with a vertical rise of 300 feet, could carry 2,400 skiers per hour.

More foreclosed and regained ownership of the area in 1993. For a number of reasons, Tamount was unable to continue to make payments on its loan. It was also unable to attract the investment capital needed to expand snow making and to make other improvements. After regaining ownership of the area, More's Table Mountain Ski Lifts, Inc. invested more than $360,000 to refurbish the area. It purchased new equipment, overhauled lifts and improved snow making.

The snow-making system at Ski Sunrise was small, and the lack of snow making eventually took its toll on the area. By early 2001, Ski Sunrise had only been able to open thirty-five days over the previous two years. Skier numbers had dropped from 12,000 during the 1997–98 season to 750 the next. And the success and proximity of Mountain High also had an effect on skier numbers. Bob Roberts, executive director of the California Ski Industry Association, noted that More "had a lack of snow and a lack of capital. He had a cute little lodge but not that much terrain, and he didn't have the snowmaking. Mountain High became extraordinarily popular, and you can't play the game when customers are stopping before they get to your doorstep."[86]

More owned and operated Ski Sunrise for more than fifty years. In the years leading up to his death on June 10, 2006, he felt it was time for someone younger to take over ownership. In its heyday in the 1960s and 1970s, Ski Sunrise provided families a small and inexpensive place to ski and was often much less crowded than other more popular local areas. But as More became older and less hands-on, the area declined due to a lack of continuity with area managers and insufficient capital investment in the area. Ski Sunrise was really a hobby for More or, as he once described it, his "alter ego career."[87]

In November 2004, Mountain High, operating what used to be Holiday Hill and Blue Ridge, purchased Ski Sunrise. The purchase included approximately one hundred acres, with one chairlift and the historic 6,000-square-foot day lodge. Resort owners renamed the area Mountain High North. However, the area remained closed until January 2008, when it was finally able to open after two feet of natural snow blanketed the area. Then, in 2011–12, management

A variety of old tow structures and buildings still adorns the slopes at Ski Sunrise. The remains of an old rope tow evoke the area's historic past.

renamed it North Pole Tubing Park. It now operates as a snow play area only, laying claim to the largest tubing park in Southern California. When the area is fully operational, there are fourteen tubing lanes and two 450-foot moving carpets to transport tubers to the top of the hill.

At North Pole Tubing Park, the classic ski chalet still graces the parking lot, and the old quad chairs hang empty, historical remnants of an area that was home to one of Southern California's first rope tows and a longtime family-owned ski resort that served generations of Southland skiers.

Kratka Ridge

In 1950, Kratka Ridge, located approximately fifty miles from Los Angeles on the Angeles Crest Highway near Mount Waterman, was developed by eleven members of the San Gorgonio Ski Club.[88] For many years, starting in the 1940s, these skiers spent many weekends skiing and exploring the area. The group members initially built a warming hut and tow for their friends and families. It was north of the existing area, across Angeles Crest Highway, with parking at the top and the rope tow stretching down the canyon. Club members eventually decided to develop their ski area as a commercial enterprise. Since the group included engineers, electricians, a contractor, an attorney and financial experts, it was just a matter of time and money to get the project off the ground. The team possessed most of the skills necessary to get the work done.

The first application for a Special Use Permit for Kratka was submitted to the Forest Service on March 4, 1948.[89] That application was submitted by the San Gorgonio Upski Company, whose name was later changed to the Angeles Winter Development Corporation to better reflect the mission of the organization. Five individuals made up the San Gorgonio Upski Company: John H. Belchee, Robert E. Dunne, Everett Lehman, Allan T. Powell and Howard Worthing.

A revised and supplementary application for the development of Kratka Ridge was filed on May 16, 1949. The group wrote:

> *Further study of the Kratka Ridge area by the original five applicants has resulted in the conclusion that their original plan in respect to the actual development was too limited in scope, and not only was a more comprehensive development required, but that a larger and more completely implemented organization was required to insure the proper and adequate development of the area. Additional members, thus increasing the financial potentiality,*

> *have been added to the organization and a name more representative of its purpose has been selected. This application is not, therefore, one by a new and different group but is a revised and augmented application supplementary to the original application of March 4, 1948 filed by the original five applicants herein above mentioned.*[90]

The group felt that ski area development should proceed progressively over a five-year period, with the first and second years as exploratory and experimental. The group explained:

> *While the area has obviously a high winter use potential unlike Snow Valley and Big Pines, it has not been extensively used. Its detailed characteristics are not fully known. Experience gained under winter conditions alone will answer certain questions. A winter use may indicate changes in the plan or program which will result in a better and more efficient development. Experience at Aspen and Sun Valley revealed that original plans required a great deal of modification and change. Lifts were relocated at Sun Valley and original plans proven inadequate. Aspen required much clearing in areas which were not originally deemed usable. These changes, however, only became apparent after winter use.*[91]

The Forest Service approved the Special Use Permit in 1950. Then the attorney in the group drew up a business plan. This marked the birth of the Angeles Winter Development Corporation and the beginning of Kratka Ridge. Each member agreed to contribute an equal amount of money and a minimum of two hundred hours of labor in the first year of construction. Enthusiasm ran high as the project began, and as it turned out, each man put in an average of seven hundred hours that year, in spite of having full-time jobs.

The Skier provided a telling description of the work and dedication that went into the initial development of the area:

> *Muscle, vision, money and dynamite have brought the Kratka Ridge project to near completion. The Angeles Winter Development Corporation, a truly cooperative organization, is composed of ten business men who donate equal quantities of time, money and backbreaking labor in an effort to beat the snow.*
>
> *After a hard day at the office, members of the organization relax evenings at bull-dozing and dynamiting. For relief they install foundations and towers.*[92]

Workers put the finishing touches on the Kratka day lodge, fall 1950. Each of the eleven members of the Angeles Winter Development Corporation put in an average of seven hundred hours of work when development of the area began. *Photo by Wolfgang Lert.*

Randy Zimmer, one of Kratka's original developers, working on the handmade stone patio next to the day lodge, fall 1950. Zimmer also managed the area for the first four years. *Photo by Wolfgang Lert.*

When the area opened for its inaugural season in 1950–51, four rope tows operated, three of which were 1,100 feet long. The fourth was a 400-foot beginner tow. There was also a stylish lodge that included a first aid room, a lounge and a kitchen to provide meals and drinks to hungry skiers. The group named the area Kratka Ridge for John Kratka, an early mountain man who hiked extensively in the area.

The eleven club members who founded the Angeles Winter Development Corporation and worked so hard to see their dream realized were John H. Belchee, a trust officer; Joe Diener, a construction superintendent; Robert E. Dunne, an attorney; Page L. Edwards, a construction engineer and superintendent and president of the group; Frank H. Ferguson, an attorney; Everett Lehman and Allan T. Powell, studio electricians; W. Woodruff Toal, a salesman for a hardwood lumber company; Rex Wakefield, an accountant; Howard Worthing, a mechanical engineer and designer; and Randy Zimmer,

Left to right: W. Woodruff Toal, Edward T. Hensley, Howard V. Worthing, Everett Lehman and Charles K. Jewell. Toal, Worthing, Lehman and Jewell were among the original eleven founding members of Kratka Ridge. Hensley came on board in 1960 and was involved in the management and development of Kratka Ridge for more than thirty years. *Courtesy of the Hensley family.*

a carpenter-contractor. Between them, this group could claim ninety-plus years of skiing experience. Bob Brambach became Kratka's first ski instructor, followed by Doug Pfeiffer for the next two seasons.

Seeking further upgrades to Kratka, the corporation soon decided to build and install a chairlift. Worthing and Diener visited every area in Southern California that had a chairlift to survey the best features of each, and Randy Zimmer traveled to Switzerland, where he spent two months studying lifts. The developers wanted to combine the best features for the Kratka chair. Worthing's sheet metal shop fabricated all of the equipment for the lift, including the bull wheel, chairs and towers.

Construction began in 1953. Area owners tackled the arduous job of clearing the land, erecting lift towers and building the upper terminal. Extensive planning went into the chairlift, and the job was described as "an original do-it-yourself project with all members pitching in until the job was completed in December 1954."[93] The two-thousand-foot single chair was equipped with seventy chairs and powered by two Chrysler engines, with one for a backup. The bull wheel, including power units, weighed five tons. The chair had a seven-hundred-foot vertical rise and a capacity of five hundred skiers per hour. In 1957, the chairlift was outfitted with a new, more powerful motor, increasing lift capacity to six hundred skiers per hour.

Skiers ride Kratka's historic single chair after Mother Nature delivered plenty of fresh snow to the slopes. *Photo by Cecil Charles.*

In 1960, Ed Hensley became mountain manager at Kratka Ridge. Born in April 1931 in Colton, California, he grew up on the small family farm. He was drawn to the mountains, and in 1949, he and his older brother Bob began to explore and seek part-time work in the Angeles National Forest. In the winter of 1952, he started working weekends and holidays for Lynn Newcomb Jr. Newcomb's father, Lynn Newcomb Sr., founded Mount Waterman, building the first rope tow there in 1939 and Southern California's first chairlift in 1942 (chairlift construction began in August 1941). Newcomb Sr. died in 1945, leaving his widow, Livona, and Newcomb Jr. to assume management of the area.

In 1959, Newcomb hired Hensley to manage Newcomb's Ranch Inn, a small hotel, restaurant and bar that served skiers and mountain visitors, and to assist at the ski area. Hensley, with his wife and three small children, moved into the inn. Shortly thereafter, Newcomb and Hensley parted ways, and during the 1959–60 season, Howard Worthing offered Hensley the mountain manager position at Kratka. Hensley accepted on the condition that he was made an equal stockholder of the Angeles Winter Development Corporation over a short period of time.[94]

So in the spring of 1960, the Hensley family moved to Kratka and took residence at the upper warming hut. This move seemingly brought good luck to the area. Ray Hensley described the good fortune that took place after their arrival:

> *What was so striking about our first 1960–61 winter season at Kratka Ridge was that it was one of the best snow ski years ever witnessed in the Angeles. It seemed to snow every week with new powder and not too much to close the roads. The new snow would come on weekdays and the weekends would be clear and sunny at the ski area. The ski area did so well that the owners agreed to help Ed build the Hensley family a three bedroom addition to live adjacent to the single chairlift building and above The Tap Room that summer. The following winter was also good and the Angeles Winter Development Corporation built a new main lodge that still exists today that included owner's quarters, expanded food service, full service ski rental and repair shop, ski patrol emergency facility and overnight quarters, and ski school overnight quarters.*[95]

This move also signaled the beginnings of the Hensley family's thirty-three-year reign at the helm of Kratka Ridge. Ray Hensley described the truly hands-on work that shaped and molded the resort: "Ed ran the food services and oversaw maintenance and repair during this last era. I became the hands-on guy as Ed got older. I groomed all night, cleared ski runs, blasted rocks,

The Hensley family, *left to right*: Ed, Ray, Mary, Tom and Linda. According to Ray, Ed was the brains and brawn, while Mary was the matriarch to all. Ray, Tom and Linda pitched in where needed and filled their free time with skiing, all three becoming accomplished competitive racers. The Hensley family managed and led the growth of Kratka Ridge for thirty-three years. *Courtesy of the Hensley family.*

replaced chairlift engines overnight, built new chairlifts, etc. Tough work and a labor of love. We always referred to ourselves as snow farmers. Or, Kratka being a very expensive hobby."[96]

By the mid-1970s, Kratka Ridge had grown to six rope tows, the two-thousand-foot single chair and a day lodge but remained small and was one of the few areas in Southern California that continued to survive with no snow making. Kratka was a lively and vibrant area during this time. Fred Burri, the yodeler for Disneyland's Matterhorn Mountain ride, entertained skiers on weekends and holidays with his traditional Swiss accordion and yodeling. The area had its own ski club and race team with a membership of more than fifty skiers.

Then, in 1983, Ray Hensley and Jim Morning bought Kratka. They were at the helm for one successful season, but then the deal fell through. The Angeles Winter Development Corporation reclaimed the area and settled with Morning.

By the mid-1980s, the struggles of a Southern California ski resort without snow making became evident. With liability insurance totaling more than $30,000 per year, payable whether the area operated or not, compounded by a season with no snow and thus no income, the days of the ski club–operated or mom-and-pop ski area were things of the past. Ray Hensley commented, "It boils down to the ski areas with snow-making usually have no problems, but the rest of us do. Last year [1986] we were open for 20 days and the year before 18. Three years ago was a pretty good season, but the year before that we were not open for even one day of skiing."[97]

In 1988, Ray Hensley began working with the Forest Service on a snow-making plan. But, as with many other Southern California areas, environmental roadblocks slowed or put an end to some projects. Forest Service officials and the U.S. Fish and Wildlife Service would not allow Kratka to use water from a stream where the mountain yellow-legged frog resided. Many scientists felt that the frog should be on the endangered species list. After hearing the bleak news, Hensley said his facility "may soon need to be listed as an endangered species as well. Either make the snowmaking happen or we might as well shut down."[98]

The snow-making plan at Kratka was a practical one. The water for snow making would be taken from the local watershed, with about 65 percent being recycled when the snow melted. The plan would require the renovation of a dam on Little Rock Creek and reconstruction of a pipeline that had been used for years to supply water to highway workers who lived at an encampment in the area. Hensley explained that the only time that water would be pumped from the creek would be during rainstorms.

It took eight years from the inception of the snow-making plan for the Forest Service to become concerned about the fate of the frog. Michael J. Rogers, supervisor of the Angeles National Forest at the time, admitted that there had been some delays in dealing with the frog issue but that they were very concerned about the effect the snow-making development would have on the frog habitat.

Rogers explained that the dam renovation would destroy vegetation along the streambed where the approximately fifteen frogs lived. Fish and Wildlife Service officials would not approve the idea of piping water from the frog habitat. They stated that "the proposal will result in significant adverse impact" to the frogs.[99] However, Mark Jennings, a Fish and Wildlife Service biologist familiar with amphibians and reptiles in the Angeles National Forest, was open to negotiation. He was in favor of the mountain yellow-legged frog gaining threatened or endangered status but also felt that the individuals involved could arrive at an agreeable resolution to the problem. "If the resort could modify the pipeline to take water further downstream, then I felt that would not bother the frogs," he said.[100] In the same breath, he mentioned that some protection must be given to the frogs. The Forest Service felt the solution to the problem was to develop an alternative water supply through wells.

The Forest Service's alternative plan required Kratka to spend more money. Hensley said the area had already spent $150,000 on consultants and studies and had no more money to invest in the project.

Even into the 1990s, skiers visiting Kratka Ridge discovered an old-school experience. The area hadn't changed much over the years. There were no gondolas, no speedy triple or quad chairs, no fancy bars, condos or hotels.

> *Instead, there is just one rope tow and two simple chairlifts. A few batten-board buildings house a tiny lift-ticket booth, a simple restaurant and caretaker's quarters. And there's an outdoor stone fireplace surrounded by picnic tables made from the hand-hewn timber of a tree that fell decades ago on the mountain. At elevations ranging from 6,800 feet to 7,500 feet above sea level, 13 runs are spread over 85 acres of rugged public land, forested by incense cedar, white fir, sugar pine, and Jeffrey pine.*[101]

In 1994, Sam Sarcinelli approached Ray Hensley about buying the ski area for his daughter and son-in-law. He purchased all of the Angeles Winter Development Corporation stock for $325,000, and John and Jacqueline Steely became the new owners of Kratka Ridge. They renamed the area Snowcrest and had ambitious plans to create a more high-profile area. The Steelys hired Ray Hensley to assist in the expansion and development of the area.

The new owners intended to add snow making, ski lifts, toboggan runs, ice skating, snowboard features and cross-country ski trails. Generating excitement for the future possibilities at Kratka, a press release claimed, "Once complete, Kratka Ridge should fulfill the dream of ski enthusiasts across Southern California who wish to swim in the morning, work in downtown Los Angeles during the day and ski in the evening, only one hour away by car. With a population base of many millions of residents, LA is one of the largest sports industry and ski resort areas in the United States."[102]

Unfortunately for Southland skiers and the new owners, their plans were not realized. During the winter of 1996–97, they installed snow making on about 25 percent of the terrain at Snowcrest. Unhappy with the performance of the equipment, they removed it after only one year of use.

Sadly, Mother Nature also didn't cooperate. John Steely recalled, "It was very difficult. We had four of the toughest years in 20 years, and all of our capital went into keeping the business alive."[103]

In 1999, a group of Southern California businessmen purchased Mount Waterman and Snowcrest. The group initially went by the name Mount Waterman Acquisition Holdings, but the name was later changed to Angeles Crest Resorts (ACR) to reflect the group's ownership of both areas. The group was made up of Barry Stubblefield, his brother Gregory Stubblefield, Jim Newcomb and Chuck Ojala, director of mountain operations.

They had bold plans to combine the two resorts, add sixteen or seventeen new chairlifts, develop extensive snow making, construct new buildings and add new rental equipment. Mount Waterman and Kratka, about three miles apart, could be linked by developing the 80 to 100 acres between the two resorts. That would add an additional 300 acres to the 150 at Waterman and the 58 skiable acres at Kratka. According to Barry Stubblefield, chief executive officer of ACR, "Five to 10 years and $75 million later and we'll have it done, but that's a wild guess."[104]

But they knew, first and foremost, that the key to reviving both areas would be the addition of extensive snow making. During that first season, 1999–2000, ACR created a snow play area that retained the Snowcrest name, while the ski and snowboard section of the mountain returned to the name Kratka. The group eventually dropped the Snowcrest name and changed it back to Kratka, and by February 2000, the first phase of snow making was near completion. The system was laid out to cover the snow play and beginners' area.

Continued installation of snow making was contingent on many factors: Forest Service approval, availability of water, difficulty of pumping water to the top of the mountain and the creation of a new reservoir. As previous owners had found, the approval process could be slow and difficult.

The initial enthusiasm and optimism of ACR was short-lived. Beginning in early 2001, a chairlift remained inoperative for months. Then, in the summer of 2001, ACR was cited for operating without a permit. Finally, in December, the lift was completely lost in a fire. This began a cycle of disputes with the Forest Service, and over the next four years, ACR often lacked the permits, as well as sufficient snowfall, necessary to operate Kratka and neighboring Mount Waterman.

In January 2005, Stubblefield, the dynamic spirit behind ACR, was killed when he fell and slid out of control into a tree while skiing in icy conditions at Mount Waterman. Friends described Stubblefield as "the motivating forces behind ACR,"[105] and without him, the corporation came to a standstill.

Then, in June 2006, with the Forest Service ready to shut down Mount Waterman and Kratka Ridge for good, real estate businessman Rick Metcalf, with his brother Brien and two other investors, jumped at the chance to purchase both areas from ACR. Metcalf had been interested in purchasing the areas when they were sold to ACR in 1999 and now had a second chance at owning both resorts. He admits, "I dove in headfirst without thinking it all through." A list of things he didn't expect were "mountain people with quirky personalities; everything that goes into the chairlifts, from the bullwheels to

Kratka's historic single chair hangs idle in this summer 2011 photograph. One of only three single chairlifts remaining in the United States, it harkens back to a simpler time of the family-owned ski area when ski lifts and buildings were the result of the labor and sweat of ski area creators.

the whisker switches; all the brakes and the emergency things, load testing... the kitchen..."[106]

As of the summer of 2012, Kratka remains closed, eleven years after its last season of operation. Kratka's historic single chair still rises to the top of the area, one of only three single chairlifts remaining in the United States. The other two single chairs—one at Mad River Glen in Vermont and the other at Mount Eyak in Alaska—still operate. Metcalf has been focused on reviving and upgrading neighboring Mount Waterman. His brother Brien, commenting about Kratka, said that they "don't have the time or resources for it, so it's staying in limbo."[107] Their current plan is to operate a tubing and snow play area and, after a number of years, install a new chairlift and open the area for skiing again. Hopefully, the historic single chair can be revived and survive another fifty or more years.

Chapter 5

MOUNT SAN JACINTO AND IDYLLWILD

Russ Leadabrand, longtime columnist for *Westways* magazine, wrote in his *Guidebook to the Sunset Ranges of Southern California*, "The San Jacinto Mountains of Riverside County elbow boldly out into the Colorado Desert, yet there are 10,000-foot peaks here and winter snows can be heavy."[108] The most dominant peak, Mount San Jacinto, is a 10,804-foot massif that towers over the town of Idyllwild and is best known for its aerial tramway. The revolving tram car transports mountain visitors via a ten-minute ride from 2,643 feet at the Valley Station near Palm Springs to the Mountain Station at 8,516 feet. This chapter will not provide an in-depth history of the Palm Springs Aerial Tramway, since its primary use is not skier transport nor is it a lost ski area.[109] However, this chapter will look at the tows that skiers utilized in and around the community of Idyllwild and on the lower slopes of Mount San Jacinto.

Nevertheless, it is interesting to examine some of the pro-skiing arguments put forward by proponents of construction of the tramway. In January 1939, the *Palm Springs Limelight* discussed the importance of the winter tourist business and felt that, with the addition of the Palm Springs Aerial Tramway, the town could compete with Sun Valley, Idaho. The newspaper suggested that winter sports might be suitable on Mount San Jacinto, that Round Valley was "a perfect ski country" and that Hidden Lake might be an "ice skaters' paradise."[110] In the spring of 1940, Modjeska and Masters, a New York engineering company, conducted a seven-week snow survey. It concluded that San Jacinto offered skiing "as good as the best" available at existing ski resorts in Southern California.[111]

Those in favor of the tramway were promoting the area based on its potential as a prime ski area: "The aim of the ski lift would be to make the long reaches and slopes of the upper regions available to all those who love the sport. If such a lift were installed, proponents of the plan point out, the San Jacinto Mountains would become the mecca for hundreds of winter sports enthusiasts who now go to the San Bernardino Mountains."[112]

For several years prior to this time, skiers had already been exploring the potential for skiing in the vicinity of Idyllwild. Most publicity and press on local skiing focused on Mount Baldy, San Gorgonio, Keller Peak and Big Pines. San Jacinto was mentioned occasionally but was not popular with most skiers. In 1934, Walter Mosauer wrote, "Idyllwild, a popular mountain resort on the massif of the San Jacinto Mountains, permits of some good skiing, especially on Tahquitz Peak (8,826 ft.); but generally the country is either too flat and level, or too abruptly dropping, broken, and rocky to be called ideal. Mount San Jacinto itself does not seem to be a good skiing mountain, because of the great horizontal distance covered in its ascent."[113]

In spite of the varying opinions regarding the suitability of Mount San Jacinto's geography for skiing, the first bill presented to the state legislature in 1939 aimed to establish a "Palm Springs Winter Park Authority" for the purpose of constructing the tramway and developing a winter sports resort. The backers of the bill emphasized "the truly unique opportunities for winter sports that the high country of San Jacinto offered."[114]

A later bill, proposed in 1945, stated, "There is in the state park system Mt. San Jacinto State Park, which is owned by the state and which is ideally situated for winter sports, including skiing, tobogganing, sledding, and skating, and which affords unlimited opportunities for healthful recreation in a snow area immediately adjacent to the desert recreation of Palm Springs."[115]

Interestingly enough, skiers themselves did not support the project. In an article in *The Skier*, the official publication of the California Ski Association, Andrew Hauk, vice-president of the association, and Lute Holley, chairman of its Area Development Committee, wrote that San Jacinto did not have the suitable terrain necessary for a ski area. Hauk and Holley based their assessment on a survey and report issued on October 7, 1946, by the Southern Area Planning Committee of the California Ski Association and the Winter Sports Committee of the California State Chamber of Commerce. They further commented in *The Skier*:

> *After on-the-spot study, the experts who prepared this report, report that the terrain of San Jacinto is extremely rugged, the west slope being heavily timbered and the north, east, and south slopes dropping precipitously from rocky, knife-edge ridges to an upland shelf scarred with ravines and giant boulders, whence it catapults over immense precipices to the desert floor 8,000 feet below. Moreover, the steep and rocky upper 1,500 feet is absolutely unskiable.*

> *The only potentially available ski terrain in the entire San Jacinto area is the rough, partly open slopes between the 8,000- and 9,000-foot levels, approximately 500 feet above and below the level of the upper terminal of the proposed tramway. But these slopes are two miles distant from the terminal, necessitating further transportation facilities not presently planned. There are no up-ski facilities on these slopes nor are any planned. And most importantly, these slopes which face south and southeast require a minimum of 6 feet of snow for safe skiing, a depth which rarely occurs even after heavy snowfalls.*[116]

Many skiers had openly criticized the proposed tramway but none so concisely as Hauk and Holley in their statement:

> *This project, according to reliable winter sport surveys, by the very nature of its location can never be anything more than a sightseeing attraction. By no sound measure can it ever be a practical skiing development. As those familiar with the area know, Mt. San Jacinto (elevation 10,805 feet) rises out of the desert adjacent to Palm Springs, and while much frequented by campers, tourists, and mountaineers during the summer months, it is by no stretch of the imagination an ideal or even suitable ski area.*[117]

In early 1949, Ralph Accardi, Johnny George, Dick Shideler and Ernie Maxwell completed a high-altitude snow survey and described the difficult terrain they encountered: "There is no easy approach to the backcountry. Sunny southern slopes were frozen and northern slopes too steep to hang to safely. Along the ridge beyond the Peak, a rope was brought into use to prevent anyone from rolling halfway to Idyllwild."[118]

The tram opened to much fanfare in September 1963, and in spite of the previous reports detailing the shortcomings of the surrounding terrain for skiing, two months later, the Mount San Jacinto Winter Park Authority retained American Crane and Hoist Corporation of Downey to study and prepare a plan for winter sports facilities at Long Valley near the Mountain Station. American Crane and Hoist hoped to secure the winter sports concession to build and operate portable rope tows, toboggan and sledding areas, ice skating and warming huts. Its proposal was subject to the approval of the Winter Park Authority and the California Department of Natural Resources.

American Crane and Hoist enlisted Economics Research Associates to conduct an economic feasibility study. It hired Willi Schaeffler, a German American ski champion and instructor, to assist in its assessment. Schaeffler was often called upon to determine the geographic suitability for ski area developments and was involved in feasibility studies for Pike's Peak, Mineral King and other California locations. The study was completed in February 1964, but details were not made public. However, it was known that the survey concluded that additional land for development would be needed and extensive clearing and grading of slopes would be necessary to create ski runs.

The desire for more land led the Winter Park Authority to submit a request to Governor Edmund Brown for use of additional forest land from the summit of Mount San Jacinto to Hidden Lake. The original tramway contract limited land use to two sections in the wild area and prohibited damage to vegetation or alteration of the land. Since the best ski terrain lay outside the existing Winter Park Authority boundary, it asked for four additional sections of land next to the two it already had in the state park. The plan was to clear five ski runs and build two ski jumps.

It is curious that the Winter Park Authority proposed such an extensive plan since its original contract stipulated that no permanent winter sports facilities, such as chairlifts, towers and buildings, could be built. It is also curious that it was planning to build ski jumps. Ski jumping had long before declined in popularity, and the jumps likely would have been little used.

Had the Winter Park Authority's request been approved, terrain subject to development would have included the top of Mount San Jacinto, its south slopes, Jean Peak, Cornell Peak, Round Valley, Desert View and Hidden Lake.

In April 1964, Norman Wilson, a snow and avalanche expert for the California Division of Parks and Beaches, spent eight days skiing the slopes from Mount San Jacinto to Hidden Lake. He submitted a negative report regarding the possibility of ski development. The *Town Crier* reported, "Conditions which the skier found to be unfavorable for winter sports development were variation in slopes which causes icy, windy conditions on Mt. San Jacinto, inferior slopes and high cost of manicuring the slopes for suitable ski runs."[119] In addition, Wilson added that ski facilities could be built near the Mountain Station, but the cost would be much higher than the estimates made by American Crane and Hoist.

By December 1964, the Winter Park Authority's ambitious plan for ski facilities had been denied, and it submitted a new request to construct a "hillalator" and a single ski tow near Mountain Station. The hillalator, or moving sidewalk, would transport tram riders from Mountain Station to Long Valley, a distance of about 370 feet, providing easier access to a nearby snow play area. The ski tow would have been built to the southwest of Long Valley. Winter sports facilities were allowed under the legislative act that created the Winter Park Authority, but only within the confines of specific sections of the state park.

So the 1946 assessment of the mountain as a sightseeing attraction and not a prime ski area proved to be accurate. In the almost fifty years that the tram has been operating, cross-country skiers and adventurous ski mountaineers have accessed the upper slopes of the mountain via the tram, but the area was never developed as a ski area. As more a novelty than anything else, a small rope tow was built near Mountain Station in the 1990s and was removed in about 2000.

In the mid-1940s, all the talk and publicity about a new ski resort in combination with the planning of the tram station at Long Valley motivated the management at Hidden Lodge to lure Tommi Tyndall from Sun Valley, Idaho, to organize and manage its winter sports program. His 1946 arrival signaled the beginning of a dedicated winter sports program for the town of Idyllwild.

Ernie Maxwell, longtime Idyllwild resident, founded Idyllwild's newspaper, the *Town Crier*, in October 1946. The second issue, dated November 16, 1946, featured a winter sports story and announced Tyndall's arrival to town:

> *Although no Los Angeles papers carry any news about the snow conditions at Idyllwild,* Town Crier *will take the bull by the horns and state the*

The bottom of the O'Conner rope tow that was installed near Mountain Station sometime in the 1990s. It was removed around 2000.

A view of the Mountain Station ski school building that served the small rope tow area, circa 1999.

obvious—that there was, and is, plenty of snow in this neighborhood! At its height, it ran all the way from 9 inches in the Village to a depth of several feet on the peaks.

So the time is here for winter sports fans from below to try their ski prowess and romp in the snow and hurl snowballs at one another—and we on the mountain, will gladly join them if we get through with our shoveling before dark!

But with all the added labor that comes with snowtime, it's a privilege to live in a scene of such quiet beauty. The boughs of the smaller pines curtsey to the ground, laden with the white magic. Pulling our sled homeward one moonlit night, we came upon ski tracks and followed them to our door. There written in bold letters in the snow was the exuberant announcement, "Tommi was here!"

Shortly after his arrival, Tyndall formed the Mount San Jacinto Winter Club, and J.J. Berkeley's Hidden Lodge became the temporary headquarters for the club. Tyndall, club president, served as the recreational director for the lodge and operated a ski school.

During the 1946–47 season, Tyndall announced that the local ski facilities would be better than ever before. Hidden Lodge blasted rocks and cleared stumps to ready its slopes for anxious skiers. The 1,700-foot ski tow at Hidden Lodge started at an elevation of 6,200 feet and topped out at 7,050 feet. Skiers had their choice of ten runs, five cross-country ski trails and a four-lane toboggan course. The main run was three-quarters of a mile long. After making a test run, Tyndall estimated that expert skiers could negotiate it in forty seconds. This run was dubbed the Gold Ski Course because Mount San Jacinto Winter Club members would use this run to vie for the Gold Star emblem.

In the fall of 1947, J.J. Berkeley left Idyllwild to focus on his business interests in Los Angeles. A group of Idyllwild residents purchased the concessions from Hidden Lodge. Jo Kun (Jo later married Tyndall and would manage Snow Summit after Tyndall's death) was in charge of the restaurant, Mary Duffield oversaw cabin rentals, Tyndall operated the ski school and Donald Smith ran the toboggan concession.

Tyndall also began dividing his time between Idyllwild and Moonridge Meadows in Big Bear Lake. Jim Neely—a California Ski Instructor Association–certified teacher—and recent Norway import Anders Swanstrom operated the Hidden Lodge Ski School in Tyndall's absence.

In January 1948, the *Town Crier* announced, "If you can't bring the snow to the ski-tow, you take the ski-tow to the snow!"[120] Tyndall and Garth Patton began using an army surplus weasel to transport skiers to higher, snow-covered elevations. The weasel left Lookout Café in Pine Cove every hour on the hour. When there was plenty of snow at Hidden Lodge, the weasel operated there.

Tyndall's stay in Idyllwild lasted little more than a year. The unreliable snow conditions at Idyllwild led him to seek out the higher elevations at Big Bear Lake. He arrived in Big Bear Lake sometime in 1948 and immediately formed his Mill Creek Ski Schools. Jo Tyndall wrote, "He was already deeply engrossed in studying the possibilities of establishing his own business using the white gold in them thar hills when I met him in Idyllwild. He was convinced that a well run ski school could prosper because he felt that skiing generally was about to become big business."[121]

When Tyndall left, the Mount San Jacinto Winter Club evidently folded. So in February 1949, plans were underway to organize a ski club. Ray Patton arranged an organizational meeting on February 8 at the Idyllwild Inn. Skiers

The cover of an Idyllwild Inn brochure highlighting a variety of winter sports available near the inn.

and non-skiers from Hemet and San Jacinto were invited to attend. Glenn Froehlich was elected president; Webb Ross, vice-president; Barbara Covington, secretary; and Ray Patton, treasurer.

A few other Idyllwild residents tried their hand at building and operating ski tows. In January 1947, Pop Groom and his sons were establishing a winter sports area above Pine Cove (elevation almost seven thousand feet). They planned to have a ski tow, toboggan slide and ski rentals. Then, in January 1948, Bob O'Donnell and Lemmy Poatos purchased four acres on Marian View Drive where they cleared a large ski slope, installed two five-hundred-foot toboggan chutes and made plans to build a rope tow. O'Donnell named his area Halona Hill.

By February 1948, Idyllwild's two ski centers, Hidden Lodge and Halona Hill, were in full swing whenever snow was plentiful enough. During the first weekend of February 1948, record crowds flocked to both areas. More than 2,500 toboggan rides were logged at the Hidden Lodge toboggan slide, and skiers were swarming the slopes at O'Donnell's Halona Hill. Garth Patton stayed busy transporting skiers to and from Hidden Lodge.

The popularity of Idyllwild winter sports continued into the 1948–49 season. On the New Year weekend, Halona Hill experienced the greatest

A map illustrating winter sports areas, facilities and surrounding trails near the Idyllwild Inn.

A busy day at the Halona Hill rope tow. Founded in 1948, the tow operated until 1964. The ski slope eventually succumbed to cabin subdivision along today's Lookout Road. *Courtesy of the Idyllwild Area Historical Society.*

number of visitors up to that date. Most of its ski and toboggan equipment was in constant use. The *Town Crier* reported, "An all-electric ski tow is to be installed at Halona replacing the various contraptions used previously."[122] The electric tow was to be built and installed by Dick Cannon of Hemet.[123]

In February 1952, Frank Meadows and Glenn Frankies began operating the tow at Hidden Lodge. The Los Angeles men worked at Hughes Aircraft during the week. Slopes for all levels of skiers were available, but the tow operated on weekends only.

By 1954, Meadows was the sole proprietor of the Hidden Lodge operation and Jim Henley the only operator of Halona Hill. But by 1955, the Hidden Lodge tow was not listed in local snow reports, so Halona Hill was apparently the lone ski tow operating in Idyllwild. At some point in the mid-1950s, Jay Burton became a partner with Jim Henley at Halona Hill. But in March 1958, H.M. Willis, who operated a cabin care business, bought Burton's share of Halona Hill. The tow again changed hands when Bob Muir took over the

A recurring scene at many Southern California ski areas that received marginal snowfall. These Idyllwild skiers relax in the sun amidst the patchy snow at the base of Halona Hill. *Courtesy of the Idyllwild Area Historical Society.*

operation during the 1959–60 season. He immediately installed a larger motor so up to five persons could use the tow at one time. Unfortunately, Idyllwild's fickle weather did not cooperate, and the 1960–61 season was snowless. The tow did not operate during the 1961–62 season even though Idyllwild had its best snowpack in five years. Even when the tow wasn't running, Halona Hill was used for all manner of snow play. It is not known when the tow was retired permanently, but on January 25, 1964, even though it hadn't been scheduled to open, the tow went into operation, much to the delight of the snow sports enthusiasts who had flocked to Idyllwild for a weekend of winter fun. This may have been the last hurrah for Halona Hill and its rope tow that served Idyllwild skiers for more than twelve years.

Today, there are no ski tows operating on Mount San Jacinto or in Idyllwild. Cross-country skiers still use the tram to access winter snow, but Mount San Jacinto or Idyllwild never became the winter sports destination that many argued it could be.

Chapter 6
SAN DIEGO COUNTY

San Diego is the quintessential Southern California city, with an abundance of sunshine and a location only twenty miles from the state's southern border. This unpromising geography didn't stop the city's ski devotees from banding together to form a ski club. The San Diego Ski Club, founded in 1935, was very active in the Cuyamaca Mountains in San Diego County. It has the distinction of being the most southwesterly club in the United States and one of the oldest active clubs in Southern California. The club started with forty members, an amazing number given the year and geographic location of the club. It held its first race, a slalom, in San Diego County at Mount Laguna in 1938.

Club members had dreamed of skiing on a local San Diego County peak, so in the fall of 1938, the State Park Commission of California approved their plan to clear shrubs, rocks and stumps on Cuyamaca Mountain.[124]

Christmas Day 1938 marked the culmination of nine consecutive weekends of work that resulted in developing a small portion of the mountain into suitable ski terrain. The Forest Service supervised the clearing of brush and undergrowth, and Milton S. Jackson and Arnold Cayser served as work party leaders. When all was said and done, one thousand man-hours of labor had been contributed to the project. An average of over 20 people per weekend was involved in the work parties, with a total of 160 individuals participating.

The ski-friendly Park Commission also approved the use of the Cuyamaca Rancho Fire Guard Station for the club to use as a ski hut. The hut was located about twenty-five minutes by trail from the ski slope. A fire road provided a nice downhill run from the slope to the hut. It was outfitted with a kitchen, fireplace, water heater, toilet facilities, running water and telephone. Most of these features were luxuries that other ski huts at the time did not possess.

In 1938, the San Diego Ski Club cleared ski runs on a portion of Cuyamaca Peak. Club members spent nine consecutive weekends clearing brush and other obstacles. Then, in 1939, they built a rope tow, tow house and shed to store ski patrol equipment, shown here. *Courtesy of Karen Wullich Herbst.*

Milton S. Jackson, vice-president of the San Diego Ski Club, and Arnold Cayser, San Diego Ski Club president, were responsible for discovering the ski terrain on Cuyamaca. Their efforts resulted in the development of the slope and facilities for the club. Because of Jackson's efforts, the club resolved that the slope be named Jackson Meadow and spearheaded the effort to give that name official recognition.

One of the San Diego Ski Club's priorities was to have a rope tow on Cuyamaca. This dream was realized when the club installed a rope tow in 1939. This tow operated until the late 1950s or early 1960s.

Additional slope improvements and clearing continued over the years, described in an interesting account of the work that took place in November 1941:

> *Thrills galore were experienced by workers at Jackson Meadows last Sunday. Three large trees and two projecting rocks were blasted off the slope in a series of loud booms that sounded like a blitzkrieg. Trunks, roots and branches went flying through the air with the greatest of ease. 145 sticks of dynamite were used for the works. With all those moguls removed from the slope, skiing this winter will be lots of fun.*[125]

The San Diego Ski Club's home slopes often presented quite a challenge. The conditions on one less-than-perfect 1942 weekend were reported in the club's newsletter:

> *The weekend of Feb. 21 and 22 found nine hopefuls bunked in the back room of the Fire Guard Station, listening to the pitter-patter of rain on the roof. A sad situation. Came the dawn with more rain and more skiers. The doughty die-hards skied through rain, slush and an occasional snowflake until the slope was reduced to chocolate pudding. Fun in the snow a la Cuyamaca! Ski-Nooz is convinced that the San Diego brand of skier is the most versatile in the country. Haven't we proven that we can ski on snow, water, pine needles and mud with equal facility!*[126]

The San Diego Ski Club was also well known for its strong skiers and ski patrol activities. One of its most acclaimed and decorated members happened

Dorothy McClung Wullich, the best female skier in San Diego County in the 1930s and 1940s, was physically strong and able to hold her own among her male counterparts. On January 12, 1942, Wullich was named the first female member of the National Ski Patrol. She earned the honor through demonstrations of physical strength, first aid skills and skiing expertise on ski patrol missions with the San Diego Ski Club. *Courtesy of Karen Wullich Herbst.*

to be a woman, Dorothy McClung Wullich. She learned to ski in 1939, inspired by ski scenes in a movie she'd watched. Only three years later, on January 12, 1942, she became the first female member of the National Ski Patrol.[127]

Dorothy proved her expertise and worthiness when she, with five other members of the San Diego Ski Club (all male), skied into Cuyamaca Peak to deliver 150 pounds of food to stranded rangers. Ordinarily, vehicles would carry supplies to the lookouts where the rangers were stationed to scan the skies for enemy aircraft. However, at this time, almost three feet of snow covered the trails, which were impassable to everyone except those on skis. The San Diego Ski Club was lauded for its accomplishment, and Dorothy proved her physical strength, first aid skills and proficiency on skis. After this feat, the *American Ski Annual* reported that Dorothy won her honor as the first female member of the National Ski Patrol based on "the strength of her record as a skier" and that her "enthusiasm has surmounted the difficulties of many arduous ski safaris."[128]

Dorothy was also a talented racer, and an injury in the 1941 San Gorgonio Downhill race motivated her to become involved in ski patrol work. Describing the mishap, she recalled, "I was going too fast, I guess, and tried to check my speed—that's all there was to it. When it was all over, I had broken my right leg in five places. With six other skiers hauling me, it took four hours to get down the trail that night."[129] She was on crutches for two months, and it was during this time that Dorothy concluded that rescue techniques in the Southern California mountains needed vast improvement. To help satisfy this need, she became a member of the San Diego Ski Patrol, the first in Southern California (established in 1941), and enrolled in Red Cross first aid courses.

In 1941, three years after the National Ski Patrol had been established, there were five hundred men in the organization. The nomination of a woman was a precedent-setting move and was not an easy one to overcome. Walter H. Clemmons, section chief of the southern district of California, took up Dorothy's cause. In a letter to Charles "Minnie" Dole, founder and chairman of the National Ski Patrol, Clemmons wrote:

> *Where women skiers are possessed of unusual skiing ability and where their stamina on skis, particularly on cross-country tours, indicates that they would be able to handle the heavier demands of rescue transportation, I have felt that they should be seriously considered for a place right alongside the male members of the National Patrol. Ability in the application of first aid can, of course, be equally as efficient in the case of women as well as men, perhaps even more efficient. Other qualifications of personality, tact and interest in patrol work can be just as desirable in women. Granted that women skiers so*

completely qualified are unusual, it still seems to me that where they meet all requirements they should be awarded full honors and considerations.[130]

Clemmons concluded his letter with the following recommendation: "I would like to respectively request that the appointment of Dorothy McClung to the National Ski Patrol be fully considered at this time before rejection because of sex, even though hers might be the first woman appointment."

Dorothy received acknowledgment that she possessed all the physical and technical abilities required to be a member of the National Ski Patrol. A letter dated January 16, 1942, from the National Ski Patrol Committee proclaimed: "The National Committee takes sincere pleasure in presenting you with Special Badge Number 1 together with your Certificate of Merit. This badge is conceived as an honorary award in recognition of the certain talents that have marked you eligible to receive it." The letter went on to state, "A Special Badge has been created for you and the National Committee looks to you to carry yourself that all women skiers and young patrolmen will aspire to the honor you have been given."

She had the opportunity to again prove her worthiness of the honor when, in 1944, the San Diego division of the National Ski Patrol was called upon for a rescue on Cuyamaca Peak. This time, fourteen skiers, including Dorothy, scaled a steep slope on two trips to carry fuel to stranded men on two snowbound federal forestry lookouts. The snow was seven feet deep, and the men had only five days' of fuel remaining when the rescue team arrived.

Five cylinders of bottled gas, each weighing 140 pounds, were transported almost a mile up the snowy slopes of Cuyamaca Peak on the patrol's toboggan. The toboggan had to be hauled two and a half miles from the fire guard station on Highway 79 to the location where the cylinders had been cached by forestry crews that had bogged down in tractor-drawn sleds the previous week. The men on this rescue included Arthur Wullich, Hughes Hobart, Henry and Norbert Mandolf (father and son), Harold Stark, Anthony H. Tenbroek, Bob Seebold, Ed Bushman, Jack Hopkins, Robert Nelson, Hubert Brooks, Walter Munk and Dick Reynolds.

In January 1949, when the higher elevations in San Diego County received unusually heavy snowfall, club members were called upon for two rescue operations. Julian, the historic mining town, had been without power for three days. Authorities had difficulty negotiating the deep snow to find the break in the line. "The San Diego skiers were called upon for *snowshoes* to assist in the repair work. Despite the warnings of impending danger the group donned their trusty *skis* and led the repair party to the trouble spot."[131]

That same weekend, January 16 and 17, 1949, the club was contacted by the San Diego County sheriff. A ninety-year-old Indian was snowbound in his cabin on Volcan Mountain. The skiers made the arduous nine-hour trip, moving the man to the road on an improvised rescue toboggan. The four skiers involved in the rescues were Art Wullich, Sandy McMaster, Joe Levine and Henry Mandolf.

San Diego County's only commercial downhill ski area, Palomar Mountain Ski Area, was developed by Charles H. Darby in the fall of 1966. Based on fifteen years of snow studies, the area opened with two two-thousand-foot T-bars plus a pair of rope tows covering the beginners' slope. Just in case Mother Nature didn't cooperate, he installed enough Larchmont snow-making equipment to cover at least ten acres. The area had beginner to advanced terrain with slopes 10 to 25 percent incline. The brochure announced over ten acres of man-made snow on four runs. Darby, a La Jolla contractor, acted as president of his Palomar Mountain Corporation, with his son Martin serving as vice-president and James Murray as secretary-treasurer.

Situated a mile and a quarter south of the renowned Mount Palomar Observatory, the ski area had a number of advantageous amenities: a paved parking lot for more than one thousand cars, a day lodge with a restaurant and ski shop and a good county highway—Palomar Mountain's Highway to the Stars—for easy access to the area.

A familiar scene at 5,600-foot Palomar Mountain Ski Area. These skiers, at the base area of the rope tow, would not be skiing were it not for man-made snow. *Courtesy of the San Diego History Center.*

When Charles Darby opened Palomar Mountain Ski Area, he was confident that the area would succeed in spite of its southern location and marginal elevation. Even man-made snow was not enough to keep the area operating for more than its inaugural season, 1966–67. *Courtesy of the San Diego History Center.*

The senior Darby spoke optimistically of his new area: "Our longest run measures 3500 feet and eventually we hope to have snowmaking equipment available for this as needed. We're sheltered and cold, and even though our top elevation is only 5600 feet we've studied this area long enough to know what we're doing."[132]

Darby's daughter, Robin Howell, recalled that the ski area only operated about ten days that winter. San Diego skiers were excited about the prospect of a local ski area, and many flocked to the Palomar Mountain Ski Area when there was snow. Unfortunately, the temperatures were often too warm for snow making, and Howell recalled that there was only one snowfall that year and it was only a few inches.[133]

Chapter 7

UNIQUE AREAS

PINE NEEDLE SKI SLOPE

Born in Austria, Sepp Benedikter began skiing in 1914 at the age of three. His youth was spent ski racing and ski teaching, shaping his path for the rest of his life. He came to the United States in 1936 to work at newly opened Sun Valley. Sun Valley had the world's first chairlift, and Benedikter held the honor of being the first person to ride it. After stints in Sun Valley and Minneapolis, Minnesota, he was lured to California to teach with Cortlandt "Corty" Hill and his star-studded Wooden Wings Ski Club in the Mammoth–McGee Creek area of the Eastern Sierra.[134] During the winter of 1938, while teaching for the Wooden Wings Ski Club, Benedikter discovered that club members Hill, Bud Lighton and Stephen Avery were interested in starting a pine needle ski slope in Southern California. With their assistance and that of Tyler Van Degrift, Benedikter moved to North Hollywood and opened his Pine Needle Ski Slope on June 29, 1939. Hollywood had the first and perhaps only public outdoor pine needle ski slope in the country.

In 1930, while still in Austria, Benedikter had developed pine needle ski slopes for both ski jumping and alpine skiing, so he knew that skiing on pine needles was feasible. He had also introduced pine needle skiing at a girls' camp in Minnesota where he worked during the summer of 1938.

Newspapers all over the country wrote about the unusual "ski area," with the Birmingham, Alabama *New Age Herald* reporting:

> *This movie capital has a new winter sport, skiing on a hillside covered with pine needles. With ice skating almost everywhere on outdoor rinks the year round, Hollywood now prides itself as something of a man-made St.*

> *Moritz. The ski idea is the special baby of one Sepp Benedikter, cheery, round-faced expert, who came over from Austria a couple of years ago to teach snow sports at Sun Valley. Benedikter conducted his first pine needle ski school in Minneapolis last summer. The movie trade beckoned so the Austrian has established a much larger slope here, on the slightly colossal Hollywood scale.*[135]

The eight-hundred-foot slope, located at Lankershim and Ventura Boulevards in North Hollywood, opened at the location of the current Universal Sheraton Hotel. It took three thousand sacks of pine needles, brought from the Sierra Nevada, to cover the area. In contrast to the current densely populated locale, the scenario was quite different when Sepp built his ski slope:

> *The slope is located at the junction of two busy boulevards, near the Universal Studios, and can be seen plainly for a long distance on Ventura Boulevard. Exceptionally smooth and attractive, the hill commands a view of the entire San Fernando Valley. The slope proper has been fenced off from the surrounding pasture, and an occasional cow, startled out of her cud-chewing placidity, moseys curiously along the fence. Most of the skiers agree that this gives the slope the pastoral air of Switzerland.*[136]

Amenities included two rope tows, a ski rental shop, a ticket office, dressing rooms and a ski shop. The rental shop was owned and operated by Tyler Van Degrift, owner of Van Degrift's Ski Hut in Los Angeles. Van Degrift had a reputation for his readiness to promote the sport of skiing whenever the opportunity arose. He was the first ski retailer in the city of Los Angeles, and the Pine Needle Ski Slope lent additional advertising for the Los Angeles store and provided an additional source of income during the off-season.

Hill, Lighton and Avery saw to it that opening night received nationwide publicity. About twenty photographers from *Life*, *Look*, *Fortune*, *Vogue*, the Associated Press, the United Press and many local newspapers were on hand for the occasion.

Numerous celebrities attended the rollicking grand opening, among them Henry Fonda and his family; the Gary Cooper family; Mr. and Mrs. Robert Taylor; Claudette Colbert and her husband, James Cagney; Hedda Hopper; and many others. Ethel Van Degrift reported, "The photographers had a field day. It was a gala night, and certainly no ski course, even on snow, ever had a more scintillating opening."[137] Bill Southworth wrote, "This idea was intriguing to reporters who could spot more movie stars on the slopes than

Right: Sepp Benedikter, a name synonymous with skiing from the 1930s through the 1970s, developed his pine needle ski slope in June 1939. Located at the corner of Lankershim and Ventura Boulevards, the slope was covered with three thousand sacks of pine needles gathered from the Sierra Nevada.

Below: Benedikter installed two rope tows to whisk skiers to the top of his pine needle ski slope. Thanks to his reputation as a ski instructor and the proximity of the slope to Hollywood, opening night proved to be a gala affair. Numerous Hollywood personalities made it to the star-studded event, including Henry Fonda, Gary Cooper, Robert Taylor, Claudette Colbert and James Cagney.

at many a premier. This resulted in publicity for skiing in newspapers and magazines all over the world and started many new skiers on their way to the mastery of the 'wooden wings.'"[138]

Not content for the slope to be known for ski lessons and beginners only, the following month, on July 9, 1939, Benedikter hosted the First International Pine Needle Ski Tournament. Local skiers, as well as ski personalities from as far away as Norway, Switzerland, France, England, Canada, Germany and Austria, entered the race. In the men's race, Fred Iselin, Siegfried "Sigi" Engl, Dave McCoy and Count Albrecht Goertz were among the most accomplished entrants. Clarita Heath Bright, member of the 1936 U.S. Women's Olympic Ski Team, topped the women's entries, and she was the women's winner. It is unknown who won the men's race, but Dave McCoy recalled the event fondly, stating that he couldn't remember if he won or lost but that it didn't matter, only that he was happy to have participated in the race.[139] Oddly, especially

Benedikter demonstrates a gelandesprung to a pair of skiers. He felt that many people in Southern California were afraid of snow and that teaching people on a dry course in summer would help to alleviate their fear of the sport.

considering the extensive press coverage that the grand opening elicited, no Los Angeles newspapers reported the results of this ski meet.

Benedikter hosted another race, a combined Downhill and Slalom Amateur Ski Meet, on August 6. Skiers from near and far entered the race. The entry list included Gerd Blom of Norway, Avalo Graham of San Francisco, Bob Mason of Stanford University and Dave McCoy of Bishop, California. Winners in the women's race were Tish Campbell, Barbara Gauntlet and Ethel Severson, finishing first through third, respectively. The top three finishers in the men's race were Bob Mason, Bob Campbell and Jack Blackmore. Names of the first-place winners were engraved on the Hedy Lamarr and Richard Greene Challenge trophies.

Touting the advantages of his pine needle slope, Benedikter commented, "So many of the people in Southern California are just afraid of snow and don't want to go in it. By starting to ski here on a dry course, in the summertime, they become interested and lose some of their aversion to snow."[140]

The Pine Needle Ski Slope's only season of business was the summer of 1939. It was probably intended to be a summer-only operation, and Benedikter was back in Sun Valley for the winter of 1940–41. During its one summer run, with its celebrity allure and nationwide publicity, Benedikter's slope was a short-lived novelty for Southland skiers.

Ski Villa

On June 25, 1966, "the first and only year round, day and night ski resort in the United States" opened for business.[141] It was located in the hills of Carbon Canyon, 640 feet above sea level and about a forty-minute drive from downtown Los Angeles. Ski runs from easy to advanced, along with a few moguls, were covered with six-inch-square plastic tiles laid over a cement base. Commenting on the unique area, one reporter wrote, "Your first reaction upon seeing Ski Villa is one of awe. Stretching up the hillside and glistening in the sunlight is an entire blanket of white. It looks like snow and skiers say it skis like snow, but it's not snow—it's plastic bristles."[142]

Ski Villa was not large. It was only four hundred yards from the ski patrol hut at the top to the fence at the bottom. The slope was just two hundred feet wide at the top, increasing to nine hundred feet at the bottom. The area covered about seven acres and presented the skier with the same types of terrain as the real thing. One side included a steep hill, while the other provided a more gradual descent. The steep slope was sometimes set as a slalom course. Three rope tows—nine hundred, five hundred and three hundred feet long—

On June 25, 1966, the first and only year-round ski resort in the United States opened for business in the hills of Carbon Canyon, about a forty-minute drive from Los Angeles. The slope was covered with 1.5 million plastic tiles, providing skiers a surface similar to spring snow conditions. *Photo by Cecil Charles.*

transported skiers to the top. At the bottom of each rope tow, skiers slid through a mat infused with silicone, spreading a slippery coating to the base of the skis. Another silicone mat was positioned at the top of each tow to ensure a friction-free descent. The only other equipment modification needed was the addition of rubber ski pole tips, provided by Ski Villa.

Resort developer John Kramer covered the hill with tiles made of plastic bristles similar to ones produced in Japan. Kramer, a retired heating and refrigeration engineer, saw a "hill" covered with the material at a Los Angeles ski show. He had been thinking about starting some sort of recreational business and became interested in the possibility of an artificial ski slope. He traveled to Japan to meet the manufacturer but found the cost of the material and import fees to be prohibitive. While there, he visited a similar hill in Funabachi, near Tokyo. That area, 350 feet by 180 feet, had been operating for three years. When he returned to the United States, he began searching for someone to manufacture the plastic tiles locally. He contacted a plastics manufacturer and found that production costs were reasonable. Kramer hired

Marion G. "Randy" Randazzo, who manufactured the tiles and also became president of the Ski Villa Corporation.

After Carbon Canyon was chosen for the location, Kramer drew up plans, graded the hill, poured cement to lay the foundation for the plastic tiles and attached approximately 1,250,000 plastic bristle tiles. Kramer became the father of the largest man-made ski slope in the world, which eventually amounted to a total investment of $750,000.

The six-inch-square tiles were initially attached to the concrete slope with an adhesive but were later secured with nylon molly-bolts to prevent the squares from buckling. Each tile was covered with 408 thick, one-and-a-quarter-inch polypropylene bristles. Some skiers likened the surface to "mid-morning spring snow."[143]

A brochure advertising the year-round day and night skiing at Ski Villa.

The labor-intensive job of gluing or bolting 1,250,000 six-inch squares on the seven-acre ski slope prompted Randazzo to come up with a new design for the plastic tiles. He filed a patent for a new interlocking tile on July 5, 1966. In his patent application he explained:

> *It is a further object of my invention to provide an artificial ski slope structural member having a plurality of elongated plastic pins extending from one side thereof and having at one edge a pair of male flanged tabs and on an opposite edge thereof a pair of mating female sockets.*
>
> *It is another object of my invention to provide an improved artificial ski surface comprised of a plurality of plastic structural members having a large plurality of elongate plastic resilient pin elements protruding from one side thereof and opposed pairs of mating male and female flange tabs and sockets interlockingly secured to each other and adhesively secured to a smooth permanent surface constructed of concrete, wood or other material.*[144]

Randazzo's new and improved plastic tiles were patented on October 22, 1968.

Ski Villa's plastic tiles were manufactured with a resin that included ultraviolet stabilizers for weatherability. In this summer 2011 photograph, plastic tiles litter Ski Villa's slope more than forty years after its one season of operation.

An artist's rendition of Ski Villa and its amenities. Developer John Kramer made the plastic slope as much like an actual ski resort as possible, incorporating a ski lodge, ski rental and clothing shop, ski club room, ski patrol building and restaurant into the area.

Kramer also installed mercury vapor lights for night skiing. To make the area as much like an actual ski resort as possible, Ski Villa sported a ski lodge, ski rental and clothing shop, ski club room, ski patrol building and restaurant. These buildings had previously been part of Camp Kinder Ring operated by Workmen's Circle, a Los Angeles Jewish organization that operated the camp from 1928 to 1958. Each building was remodeled to look like it came directly from the Swiss Alps. The area also included a ski school, headed by John McKown, with associate ski instructors Adi Muehlegger and Elmar Fend.

The resort also catered to non-skiers. There were two swimming pools, an outdoor skating rink, a miniature golf course, a shuffleboard deck, a picnic area and horseback riding.

A local newspaper journalist reported on his experience at Ski Villa:

> *It was hard to realize that the white slippery stuff under my boards was not made of frozen water. After the inevitable falls I consciously expected wet gloves and a handful of snow down my back but alas…the only thing I collected was a blue spot on my leg. (Gloves and parkas are mandatory equipment, despite the hot sun, to prevent abrasions caused by the plastic bristles.)*
>
> *Skiing technique is about the same as on real snow. In fact, when one executes a "snow plow" skis do not catch because the snow does not plow up. Parallel technique is easily learned since the surface is so ideally uniform on any part of the hill at any time of the day. Will I try it again? You bet! The*

> *ski patrol people jokingly assured me that no frostbites will ever happen at Ski Villa. What more could a ski-bunny ask for…in September?*[145]

Ski Villa also hosted a variety of special events. In November 1966, the Southern California Ski Writers held its installation dinner meeting that was also attended by members of the Southern California Ski Tow and Lift Operators Association. A group of ten ski writers raced in the Grand Crash Slalom, held under the lights on the plastic hill. The *Far West Skier* reported the results of the novel event: "Crouched in the West Covina 'egg' position, Elmar Baxter scrambled to victory and a handsome trophy in the first annual Grand Crash Slalom on Ski Villa's broad plastic hill in Chino Canyon, near Pomona."[146]

Then, on December 4, Olympic champion Stein Eriksen made his first Southern California visit at Ski Villa. He gave a skiing exhibition, answered questions and signed autographs. His visit was sponsored by Head Ski Co. and Neal's Pro Shop. Howard Head was also at the event to introduce his new Head 360 ski, which Stein then put to the test on the plastic slope. Stein commented that he "has skied about every surface imaginable from saw dust to plastic chips and found the plastic mats to be very skiable plus a lot of fun."[147]

After six months of business, Kramer summed up the character of Ski Villa: "It has proved an excellent hill for teaching beginners and for permitting the better skiers to condition themselves as well as have fun. We didn't set out to build a hill for experts and speed skiers. That's obvious when you consider our vertical rise is about 280 feet. Basically, this is for intermediate skiing."[148]

Kramer added that the area would expand as needed and that he was considering building a steeper run that would funnel onto the main hill. During the first and only season, the ski school was very busy, and fifteen ski clubs made reservations for the clubroom.

Ski Villa opened to much enthusiasm and plenty of publicity. Articles were published in many local newspapers and a variety of national magazines. After Ski Villa's first summer of operation, *Modern Plastics* reported on the progress and prospects of plastic ski slopes:

> *There have been several attempts, both here and abroad, to put plastics to use in the construction of snowless ski slopes. All these have been pretty much on a small scale. But now comes a new concept in plastics ski-slope construction that, should it find widespread acceptance, could account for a sizable portion of polypropylene sales. In fact, the developers can visualize the day when this application alone could consume all of today's polypropylene supply, although most impartial observers look at this prediction with what might mildly be called serious doubt.*

> *For the time being, however, the first plastic ski hill of the new type caught on quickly in California. All through the summer of this year, the idea of snowless skiing attracted as many as 700 skiers per day to the slope.*
>
> *So the developers are presently looking for new locations in the state. At the same time, they believe that the plastic slope will be just as popular in winter resorts, since it will take away much of the financial risk involved in unpredictable weather.*[149]

While discussing the gamble of creating a venture like Ski Villa, Kramer commented, "I know this is no ordinary business venture. It is one of those things that can make a zillion or fall flat on its face."[150] Unfortunately for Kramer and skiers who utilized the area, it fell flat on its face. Kramer had hoped that skiers would use the plastic slope when there was no snow in the local mountains. He figured he would need at least 3,500 skiers per week for Ski Villa to stay afloat.

It is not known what the weekly skier numbers were, but the novelty of Ski Villa wore off quickly, and it closed after only one year of operation. A letter to Ski Villa's creditors and stockholders, dated October 2, 1967, from Randy

The concrete slopes of Ski Villa are still visible to travelers driving through Carbon Canyon.

Randazzo's Karen Supply Company, doing business as Ski Villa, spelled out the grim financial state of affairs:

> *We regret to inform you that the lease of the seven acre ski slope has been terminated by reason of foreclosure by the Liberty Savings & Loan Association of the first deed of trust on the ski slope. In addition, the slope has consistently operated at a loss, and Ski Villa has exhausted all of its liquidated assets and borrowing capacity in an attempt to keep the slope in operation. Accordingly, the Board of Directors of Ski Villa voted to permanently shut down operations.*[151]

Ski Villa's August 15, 1967 financial statement showed a total net operating loss of $65,641.27.

So the life of the nation's only outdoor plastic ski resort was short-lived, surviving for little more than one year. Plastic tiles are still used for skiing, but in the United States, their use has primarily been limited to short-term events such as ski shows, exhibitions and ski demonstrations.

NOTES

Introduction

1. "Winter Sports Development in California: A Project of the California State Chamber of Commerce," March 1, 1932, 1.
2. Ibid.
3. Robert O. Foote, "Skis Enter Sunny Land," *New York Times*, January 24, 1937.
4. Report of the Winter Sports Committee of the California State Chamber of Commerce—Summary of Activities, 1937–1938 Season, Ethel Van Degrift Collection, California Ski Library.
5. Ethel Van Degrift, *Vacation Time*, radio program broadcast on KFWB in Los Angeles, February 24, 1939, typewritten transcript, Ethel Van Degrift Collection, California Ski Library.
6. "Winter Sports Development in California," 1.
7. *Big Bear Lake Limelight*, "Bear Valley Has Most Ski Tows in the World!" January 13, 1950.
8. Lynn Rogers, "Southland Snow Meccas Visited," *Los Angeles Times*, February 13, 1955.
9. *Pasadena Star-News*, "Small Resorts at Mercy of Mother Nature," December 3, 2002.

Chapter 1

10. Lake Arrowhead Winter Sports Brochure, n.d.
11. For more on Walter Mosauer and Otto Steiner, see Wicken, *Pray for Snow*.
12. *Los Angeles Times*, "Gorgonio Scaled by Ski Group," March 8, 1934.
13. Walt Beesley, "Ski Meet Drawings Made," *Salt Lake Tribune*, December 29, 1934.

14. Prior to his ski activities in Lake Arrowhead, Salm was a leader in building tows at Green Valley Lake. He built the first rope tow there in 1937, one of Southern California's first ski lifts. See the Green Valley Lake section.
15. Russ Leadabrand, "Let's Explore a Byway…Across the San Bernardino Mountains," *Westways*, December 1961, 5.

CHAPTER 2

16. *Los Angeles Times*, "Los Angeles Park Attracting Crowds," February 11, 1929.
17. Doris Wubben, "Green Valley Winter Sports," unpublished paper, 1993.
18. The remnants of the old automobile engine that powered Wubben's tow can still be found at the top of the run.
19. Lyle Ferguson, interview by author, Green Valley Lake, CA, March 13, 2000.
20. Ibid.
21. Diane Slezak, "Ski Green Valley Tests Snowboard-Only Days," *San Diego Union-Tribune*, January 18, 1993.
22. Mike Erickson, "Green Valley Offers Relaxed Atmosphere," *Los Angeles Times*, February 9, 1961.
23. Randy Pattison, e-mail to author, February 10, 2012.
24. Ibid.
25. Erickson, "Green Valley Offers Relaxed Atmosphere."

CHAPTER 3

26. The other two were at McGee Creek in the Eastern Sierra Nevada, built in 1937, and Fish Camp (Snow Valley), built in 1938.
27. It is unknown if Lynn was on snowshoes or skis. Skis were often referred to as snowshoes at that time.
28. J.W. Dustrude, United States Government Memorandum, Special Use Permit—Snow Forest, Inc., November 16, 1966. San Bernardino National Forest, Office of the Supervisor, Record Group 95, Records of the Forest Service, National Archives at Riverside, Perris, California.
29. For more on Edi Jaun, see the Lake Arrowhead chapter.
30. *Mountaineer*, "Upski Towers Being Erected," November 11, 1938.
31. Doug Pfeiffer, "One of a Kind—The Big Bear Sling Lift," *Skiing Heritage*, June 1998, 29.
32. *Big Bear Lake Limelight*, "Record Crowds Enjoy Skiing," November 27, 1946.
33. *Big Bear Lake Limelight*, "Ski Fans Keep Tows Busy Over Weekend," December 10, 1947.
34. *Mugelnoos*, "Ski Huts and Ski Ups," November 10, 1938, 2.

35. *Grizzly*, "Winter Sports Furnish Outing of Thrills at Big Bear," February 18, 1944.
36. 1947 National Skiing Guide, 91.
37. For a more complete biography and account of Tyndall's accomplishments, see Wicken, *Pray for Snow* and Dick Kun, *The Snow Summit Story.*
38. Dewitt Nelson, Forest Supervisor, to Regional Forester, September 10, 1940. San Bernardino National Forest, Office of the Supervisor, Record Group 95, Records of the Forest Service, National Archives at Riverside, Perris, California.
39. C.B. Morse, Assistant Regional Forester, to Forest Supervisor, September 20, 1940. San Bernardino National Forest, Office of the Supervisor, Record Group 95, Records of the Forest Service, National Archives at Riverside, Perris, California.
40. W.L. Minaker, Division of Engineering, to Regional Engineer, October 9, 1940. San Bernardino National Forest, Office of the Supervisor, Record Group 95, Records of the Forest Service, National Archives at Riverside, Perris, California.
41. DeWitt Nelson, Forest Supervisor, to Regional Forester, November 6, 1940. San Bernardino National Forest, Office of the Supervisor, Record Group 95, Records of the Forest Service, National Archives at Riverside, Perris, California.
42. William E. Young Sr., Assistant to Purchasing Agent, to United States Forest Service, June 22, 1948. San Bernardino County Archives.
43. Fearn E. Munster, "The Sitzmark," *Limelight News*, April 1, 1949.
44. Lynn was found in his apartment adjoining his court with a pistol by his side. He had been despondent over poor health. He was sixty-two years old.
45. Dedicatory Speech for Ski Lift, September 24, 1949. Written by Mrs. Underhill, editor of the *Grizzly Press*, read by Mrs. Bertha Burton. San Bernardino County Archives.
46. Big Bear Winter Club postcard, courtesy of Snow Summit.
47. C.A. Bonner, Superintendent, Safety Division, Pacific Indemnity Company, to the San Bernardino County Board of Supervisors, July 14, 1950. San Bernardino County Archives.
48. *Big Bear Lake Limelight*, "Expect to Begin Work at Once on Chair Lift," September 1950.
49. Big Bear Lake Park Board to San Bernardino County Board of Supervisors, February 16, 1950. San Bernardino County Archives.
50. *The Skier*, "Big Bear Better Than Ever," January 15, 1951, 8.
51. Bear Valley ski tow operators to the County Park Board, November 9, 1950. San Bernardino County Archives.
52. The $125,000 minimum bid was slightly more than the capital outlay for the area. Beginning with the construction of the sling lift to final work during the 1956–57 season, $113,373 had been invested in the area.

53. *Daily Sun*, "County Ski Lift Purchase Goes to 2nd Buyer Group," April 3, 1963.
54. D.M. Tucker, Recreation and Lands Staff Officer, Memo: Special Use Permits, Snow Forest, May 19, 1964. San Bernardino National Forest, Office of the Supervisor, Record Group 95, Records of the Forest Service, National Archives at Riverside, Perris, California.
55. Daniel Platus to Ronald J. McCormick, District Ranger, April 17, 1967. San Bernardino National Forest, Office of the Supervisor, Record Group 95, Records of the Forest Service, National Archives at Riverside, Perris, California.
56. Daniel Platus to Ronald J. McCormick, District Ranger, July 19, 1967. San Bernardino National Forest, Office of the Supervisor, Record Group 95, Records of the Forest Service, National Archives at Riverside, Perris, California.
57. Dan Platus to David Nelson, District Ranger, June 27, 1970. San Bernardino National Forest, Office of the Supervisor, Record Group 95, Records of the Forest Service, National Archives at Riverside, Perris, California.
58. J.W. Dustrude, United States Government Memorandum, Special Use Permit—Snow Forest, Inc., November 16, 1966. San Bernardino National Forest, Office of the Supervisor, Record Group 95, Records of the Forest Service, National Archives at Riverside, Perris, California.
59. David G. Mohla, Acting Forest Supervisor, to Regional Forester, September 18, 1978. San Bernardino National Forest, Office of the Supervisor, Record Group 95, Records of the Forest Service, National Archives at Riverside, Perris, California.
60. Michael D. Duffy, Director Fiscal Management Staff, to San Bernardino National Forest Supervisor, October 6, 1978. San Bernardino National Forest, Office of the Supervisor, Record Group 95, Records of the Forest Service, National Archives at Riverside, Perris, California.
61. *The Skier*, November 15, 1979.
62. *The Skier*, "Snow Forest Rebuilds," December 1, 1980.
63. Don R. Bauer, Forest Supervisor, to Robert B. Rigney, Assistant Administrative Officer, County of San Bernardino. San Bernardino National Forest, Office of the Supervisor, Record Group 95, Records of the Forest Service, National Archives at Riverside, Perris, California.
64. Doug Padilla, "Public Facing Avalanche of Snow Forest's Bills," *San Bernardino Sun*, February 1, 1995.
65. Glen Binford, "Ski Trails," *Los Angeles Times*, January 17, 1956.
66. *Big Bear Lake Limelight*, "Snow Making at Rebel Ridge Is Successful Chuck Smith Reports," December 28, 1956. Moonridge was the first Big Bear Lake ski area to successfully install snow making, but by the mid-1960s,

it was no longer using it. Moonridge advertised its man-made snow as "Magic Snow."

67. Bill McMains, interview by author, Big Bear Lake, CA, April 27, 2000.
68. *Skiing*, "Rebel Snow," January 1961, 47.
69. Mike Erickson, "Snow Making System Boosts Rebel Ridge," *Los Angeles Times*, December 20, 1960.
70. Man-made snow had been experimented with elsewhere in the United States. In 1950–51, Walt Schoenknecht successfully experimented with snow making at Connecticut's Mohawk Mountain.
71. Bill McMains, interview, April 27, 2000.
72. By January 1964, Rebel Ridge, Snow Summit and Snow Forest all had snow-making systems in place. The lone area in Big Bear without snow-making facilities was Moonridge.
73. *Ski World, Los Angeles Times*, "Custom Snow Planned for Nearby Areas," November 8, 1963, 9.
74. Rebel Ridge held a copyright on the term "Custom Snow." Lou Desser, "New Mexico Boasts Skier's Paradise," *Los Angeles Times*, January 6, 1965.
75. *Los Angeles Times*, "Rebel Ridge Promises Two Feet of Snow," November 4, 1966.
76. *Los Angeles Times*, "Big Bear Resort Has Designs on L.A. Skies [*sic*]," November 4, 1966.
77. Lou Desser, "New Chairlift Doubles Snow Valley's Capacity," *Los Angeles Times*, November 30, 1966.
78. *Grizzly*, "Publicizing Ski Slopes," December 10, 1948.
79. *Big Bear Lake Limelight*, "Mill Creek Ski School to Promote Winter Sports," December 10, 1948.
80. *Big Bear Lake Limelight News*, August 6, 1948.

CHAPTER 4

81. The Big Pines Ski Club is still in existence, giving it the distinction of Southern California's oldest surviving ski club.
82. Big Pines Ski Club Resolution, December 6, 1940, California Ski Library.
83. The Big Pines Ski Club later built a private rope tow adjacent to its clubhouse. It is unknown when the tow was built, but the club was attempting to sell the tow motor in 1963, and the cables and other remnants were removed in 1977. Some remnants of the upper tow pulley still remain just below Table Mountain Road.
84. Howard V. More to William V. Mendenhall, Forest Supervisor, February 8, 1945. San Bernardino National Forest, Office of the Supervisor, Record Group 95, Records of the Forest Service, National Archives at Riverside, Perris, California.

85. Howard V. More to George Armstrong, June 1, 1949. San Bernardino National Forest, Office of the Supervisor, Record Group 95, Records of the Forest Service, National Archives at Riverside, Perris, California.

86. Valerie J. Nelson, "Howard More, 91; Southland Ski Pioneer," *Los Angeles Times*, July 3, 2006.

87. Howard More, interview by author, Pasadena, CA, December 8, 1999.

88. The original permit application for Kratka Ridge lists ten members of the Angeles Winter Development Corporation. Larry Zimmer is not listed on the permit application but became involved with the area shortly thereafter. He became the eleventh member of the group.

89. "Application for Use Permit at Kratka Ridge, Mt. Waterman Area, Angeles National Forest, May 16, 1949," Howard More Collection, California Ski Library.

90. Ibid.

91. Ibid.

92. *The Skier*, "Muscle, Vision and Dynamite at Kratka Ridge," October 15, 1953, 8.

93. *Southland Skier*, "The Kratka Ridge Story," December 1, 1964, 14.

94. By 1963, Hensley had become a partner in the Angeles Winter Development Corporation.

95. Ray Hensley, e-mail to author, June 23, 2012.

96. Ray Hensley, e-mail to author, July 1, 2012.

97. Hal Snyder, "Snowed Under by High Insurance Costs: 'Mom and Pop' Resorts Might Be a Dying Breed," *Orange County Register*, December 31, 1987.

98. Berkley Hudson, "Kratka Crunch: Ski Facility's Snow-Making Project Is Snagged by a Five-Inch Frog," *Los Angeles Times*, November 28, 1993.

99. Ibid.

100. Ibid.

101. Ibid.

102. Kratka Ridge, "News Release: Los Angeles Is Gaining a New Major Ski Resort," November 10, 1994.

103. Debbie Pfeiffer Trunnell, "Businessmen Buy Family-Owned Ski Areas," *Pasadena Star-News*, December 14, 1999.

104. Dave Strege, "No Snow Doesn't Stop Sale: New Ownership of Local Resorts Plan to Add Snowmaking Equipment and Enlarge Facilities," *Orange County Register*, December 9, 1999.

105. Micah Abrams, "L.A. Story," Skinet.com. Accessed July 9, 2011. www.skinet.com/skiing/resorts/2009/09/la-story-0.

106. Ibid.

107. Tiffany Hsu, "The Revival of Mt. Waterman," *Los Angeles Times*, March 12, 2009.

Chapter 5

108. Leadabrand, *Guidebook to the Sunset Ranges*, 5.
109. For a history of the Palm Springs Aerial Tramway, see Davis, *Wilderness, Politics, and Bureaucracy* and Wicken, *Pray for Snow*.
110. Editorial, *Palm Springs Limelight*, January 14, 1939.
111. *Palm Springs Limelight*, April 27, 1940, quoted in Davis, *Wilderness, Politics, and Bureaucracy*, 160.
112. *Hemet News*, "Proposed Ski Lift Would Open Higher Altitudes of San Jacinto Mountains," January 5, 1940.
113. Walter Mosauer, "Ski Trips in Southern California," *Sierra Club Bulletin*, June 1934, 47.
114. Harry C. James, "The San Jacinto Winter Park Summer Resort Scheme," *Living Wilderness* (Winter 1949–50): 13.
115. Ibid.
116. Ibid.
117. Ibid.
118. *Town Crier*, "High Altitude Survey," March 5, 1949.
119. *Town Crier*, "Tramway Ski Plan Dimmed," April 10, 1964.
120. *Town Crier*, "A-Weaseling We Will Go," January 3, 1948.
121. Jo Tyndall, "Snow Gently, Sweet Blizzard," 45.
122. *Town Crier*, "Snow Sports Crowds Enthusiastic," January 8, 1949.
123. In 1949, Cannon built the Lynn Lift, Big Bear Lake's first chairlift.

Chapter 6

124. Cuyamaca Peak, located forty miles east of San Diego, is the second-highest point in San Diego County at 6,512 feet elevation. Hot Springs Mountain is the highest at 6,533 feet elevation.
125. *Ski-Nooz: A Bimonthly News-Sheet Published by and for Members of the San Diego Ski Club*, "Fireworks at Cuyamaca," November 26, 1941.
126. *Ski-Nooz: A Bimonthly News-Sheet Published by and for Members of the San Diego Ski Club*, "Cuyamaca Mud Fest," March 2, 1942.
127. Ethel Van Degrift, "Ski Slants," *Los Angeles Times*, April 21, 1942.
128. Langley, *American Ski Annual 1943*, 192.
129. Harold Keen, "S.D. Girl First to Qualify: Stenographer Gets Badge No. 1 After Test," *San Diego Tribune-Sun*, January 31, 1942.
130. Walter Clemmons, letter to Charles Dole, September 29, 1941.
131. *The Skier*, "San Diego Skiers to the Rescue," February 1,1949, 4.
132. *Far West Skier*, "San Diego Ski Area Open," October 28, 1966.
133. Peter Brueggeman, e-mail to the author, July 14, 2012.

CHAPTER 7

134. Wooden Wings was a star-studded club, with a roster including Hollywood greats Gary Cooper, Errol Flynn, Henry Fonda, David Niven, Tyrone Power and David O. Selznick.
135. Notes about pine needle ski slope, Ethel Van Degrift Collection, California Ski Library.
136. Ethel Van Degrift, "Pine Needles Pinch-Hitting for Snow on Hollywood Ski Run," *Sporting Goods Dealer*, October 1939, 60.
137. Ibid., 74.
138. Bill Southworth, "Sepp Benedikter," Sepp Benedikter Collection, California Ski Library.
139. Robin Morning, e-mail to the author, July 3, 2012.
140. Van Degrift, "Pine Needles," 96.
141. Wilson Turner and C. Barry Hammons, "No-Snow Skiing," *Ski*, November 1, 1966, 100.
142. Stanley H. Ireland, "Where Snow Is Old-Fashioned," *Ford Times*, July 1967, 12–13.
143. Burt Sims, "Summer Skiing in Los Angeles," *Far West Skier*, October 14, 1966, 1.
144. "Artificial Ski Surface," Patent number 3,406,617. Marion G. Randazzo, Inglewood, CA, assignor to Karen Supply Co., Inc., Chino, CA, October 22, 1968.
145. George G. Siposs, "There's Snow on This Hill," *Long Beach Independent Press-Telegram Southland Magazine*, September 25, 1966.
146. *Far West Skier*, "Grand Crash Trophy Goes to Baxter at Ski Villa," November 25, 1966, 7.
147. Bob Cartmell, "Snow Blanket for the Holidays," *Pasadena Independent*, December 6, 1966.
148. Ibid., 8.
149. *Modern Plastics*, "One Polypropylene Ski Slope=320,000 lb. of Resin," November 1966, 92.
150. Bud Tucker, "Snow-less Skiing," *Oxnard Press-Courier*, July 3, 1966.
151. Notice to Creditors and Stockholders of Karen Supply Co., Inc., a Corporation Doing Business Under the Name of Ski Villa, October 2, 1967. Charles Morse Papers, California Ski Library.

BIBLIOGRAPHY

Bellamy, Stanley E. *Running Springs*. Charleston, SC: Arcadia Publishing, 2007.

Core, Tom. *Big Bear: The First 100 Years*. Big Bear City, CA: Core Trust, 2005.

Davis, Richard C. *Wilderness, Politics, and Bureaucracy: Federal and State Policies in the Administration of San Jacinto Mountain, Southern California, 1920–1968*. Riverside: University of California, 1973.

Hatheway, Roger G., and Russell L. Keller. *Lake Arrowhead*. Charleston, SC: Arcadia Publishing, 2006.

Krig, Pat, and Barbara Van Houten. *Wrightwood and Big Pines*. Charleston, SC: Arcadia Publishing, 2004.

LaFuze, Pauliena B. *Saga of the San Bernardinos*. Big Bear City, CA: Big Bear Valley Historical Society, 2006.

Langley, Roger, ed. *American Ski Annual 1943*. N.p.: National Ski Association of America, 1942.

Leadabrand, Russ. *A Guidebook to the Sunset Ranges of Southern California*, Los Angeles: Ward Ritchie Press, 1965.

Martell, Al. "The Kratka Story." *Summit Magazine*, March 1952.

Robinson, John W. *The San Bernardinos*, Arcadia, CA: Big Santa Anita Historical Society, 1993.

Robinson, John W., and Bruce D. Risher. *The San Jacintos*, Arcadia, CA: Big Santa Anita Historical Society, 1993.

Smith, Robert B. *Idyllwild and the High San Jacintos*. Charleston, SC: Arcadia Publishing, 2009.

Wicken, Ingrid P. *Pray for Snow: The History of Skiing in Southern California*. Norco, CA: Vasa Press, 2002.

———. *Skiing in Southern California*. Charleston, SC: Arcadia Publishing, 2007.

ABOUT THE AUTHOR

Ingrid P. Wicken is an associate professor of kinesiology at Moreno Valley College. She is the leading authority on the history of skiing in Southern California and has written two books: *Pray for Snow: The History of Skiing in Southern California* (2002) and *Skiing in Southern California* (2007). She founded the California Ski Library (www.skilibrary.com) in 2005. She was awarded the Far West Ski Association's Western Ski Heritage Award in 2002 and 2005 and the International Ski History Association's Skade Award in 2003 and 2008.